GREEN GRASS
IN THE
JUNK YARD

GREEN GRASS
IN THE
JUNK YARD

HOPE FOR TOUGH TIMES

BECKY OVERHOLT & JOHN CANINE

Pleasant Word
PW A Division of WinePress Group

Pleasant Word (a division of WinePress Publishing, PO Box 428, Enumclaw, WA 98022) functions only as book publisher. As such, the ultimate design, content, editorial accuracy, and views expressed or implied in this work are those of the author.

Unless otherwise noted, all Scriptures are taken from the *Holy Bible, New International Version®, NIV®*. Copyright © 1973, 1978, 1984 by the International Bible Society. Used by permission of Zondervan. All rights reserved.

ISBN 13: 978-1-4141-1446-0
ISBN 10: 1-4141-1446-X
Library of Congress Catalog Card Number: 2009903777

To John's wife, Nanci, and Becky's husband, Steve. Their steadfast love and commitment reflect God's love.

To mom who always said we could.

CONTENTS

Friends Don't Let Friends Believe Lies
Power, Love, and a Sound Mind

INTRODUCTION

I N THE PAST, I would have never chosen to read a book like this, much less attempt to write one. I was always frustrated with the endless prayer lists I received from church whenever someone got sick and the constant updates on his or her health. I always have felt there is more to life than just drowning in the immediate problems. Health issues are just temporary delays in the course of life.

Then I was diagnosed with breast cancer.

Even after the diagnosis, I didn't want to focus on my illness. Shortly after I received the news, a woman in my church invited Sue, a good friend of mine who was undergoing treatment for HER2/positive, a very aggressive breast cancer that is less responsive to hormone treatment, and me to her house to visit with her good friend who was undergoing chemo for the second time. I didn't want to go, but I couldn't find any polite excuse to get out of it.

I left school a little earlier than usual and met the women at the designated location. This was not a tea party that I wanted to attend. The event's purpose seemed to be to encourage me that I could make it through what I was about to experience. I smiled, talked, and agreed that God meets every need, but I wanted out of there. I wanted as far away from cancer as I could get. I preferred to be with the living and the healthy. I didn't want to hear that you could make it through chemo and that losing your hair was not a big deal. I didn't want to hear that God's grace would be sufficient. I wanted to run out of the house.

Now as I write this book, I have to smile. Am I doing what those women did to me that day? Am I expecting people to read about a disease they would prefer to deny? I hope that is not the case. Rather, in these pages I want you, the reader, to find courage for living in any circumstance life offers. I want you to connect to life, enjoy human hugs, fight the fight, accept the challenge, appreciate the encouragement, look beyond life's circumstances, and always know there is something to look forward to.

I also hope that just as I have learned to reconnect with my brother through my health crisis, you will reconnect with those who matter the most to you and begin to appreciate in a deeper way family members and friends who offer their support in tough times. I hope in these pages you will be able to relate to the emotions you or a friend might experience in a similar situation. For those who are caregivers or part of a support team, I hope you will begin to understand the source of encouragement you can be to your loved one. I trust my brother's approach will be a model for your communication.

Above all, I hope you will see the reality of the spiritual struggle we face in tough times. My brother and I were raised in a pastor's home. The Bible had been an important part of our lives since before we could remember, but when I was diagnosed with cancer, no amount of "trusting" or meditating on God's Word could completely remove the struggle or the doubts. I was human. I experienced fear. I had meltdowns. I couldn't focus on verses I had embraced and quoted over the years. I questioned God's presence, I struggled with the possibility of death, and I secretly wondered what I had done to make God so mad. This is the spiritual struggle, and, in my opinion, we are not transparent in this struggle. All too often we glibly claim victory and peace that we don't actually have.

As I went through my diagnoses, surgeries and treatments, I tried to be honest with myself. Frankly, many days I did not have a positive attitude or spiritual prowess. In fact, if a positive attitude was the prerequisite for healing and spiritual living, then I would be physically dead and my spiritual life would be in shambles. But I believe God understands our humanness. I believe He walks with us through every difficulty, even when we are kicking and screaming or running wildly to avoid the inevitable.

One individual from Florida, who received my letters from a mutual friend, was a new believer in Jesus when she received news of her cancer. She was feeling guilty that she was struggling with the diagnosis. When she read my letters, she told her friend that if a pastor's wife could have these feelings, then she could accept her own struggles and not think she was going through them because her faith wasn't strong enough.

When you allow yourself to let down the walls and lead a transparent life before others, they will be encouraged by your honesty and know they are not alone in what they are experiencing. Whether you are reading to find comfort in your situation or whether you are interested in how you can help a loved one through a difficult time, I trust you will be authentic in your relationship with God. Why not? He knows what you are thinking anyway.

It has now been three years since my first cancer diagnosis. As I look back on my situation, I know I would not have chosen the path my life has taken. Being diagnosed with two cancers within two months would not be something I consider a "gift." Life is the gift God has given me; cancer is ugly. Nor will I say that the purpose of my cancer was for God to teach me. I am a teacher by profession (currently a principal), and I don't think teaching has to be painful or distasteful. I did learn from my experiences, but I will not accept that the primary reason I contracted cancer was for God to teach me. God uses all the experiences of our lives to draw us to Him—and cancer, disease, and death were never a part of His original plan.

What happened to me is only my story. God will write the story of your life. I am resigned to accept that in my situation, I may never know why I had two cancers. Likewise, you may never know why the events of your life have unfolded the way they did. I do know cancer caused me to reflect on what God's Word teaches, and I know my brother helped me define many truths for living. I loved life before cancer, I looked for ways to enjoy life during the surgeries and treatments, and I am loving life again.

There will come a day when each of us will enjoy life even more than is now possible. So as God writes the story of your life, be transparent and honest with yourself. It is my and my brother's prayer that this message of faith, hope, and love will encourage you on your journey.

SEVEN MAXIMS

1. Connect to life.
2. Enjoy hugs and home.
3. Accept the challenge.
4. Fight the fight.
5. Appreciate the encouragement.
6. Look beyond the circumstances.
7. Celebrate the future.

Chapter 1

. . . .

CONNECT TO LIFE

Often the test of courage is not to die, but to live.[1]

—Vittorio Alfieri

September Diagnosis

I T WAS THE end of summer, and I had completed my third year as principal of Tuckerton Elementary. I was anticipating a smooth start to my tenure year. At church, my husband, Steve, a pastor, and I had finished a week of vacation Bible school with more than 250 children and a hundred adult leaders. To end the summer, we were more than ready to spend some vacation time in Florida with our children, Joshua, Joanna, and Jodie, their spouses, and, of course, our grandchildren. We had planned a family get-together and rented a house with a pool outside the back-patio door. The complex also had a larger pool with a lazy river and waterslide. Everyone was ready for some fun.

We were sitting at an outside table around the complex's pool one afternoon when my cell phone rang. It was my

17

gynecologist's nurse, calling to tell me that my routine mammogram had showed something suspicious. She told me not to worry and to enjoy my vacation, but said when I returned home I should come in for a second mammogram. I followed her advice. Several turns on the waterslide, numerous rounds on the lazy river, and a trip to Sea World kept me from worry. However, on the plane ride home, I began to note dates and intervals of previous menstrual cycles and document that my body was going through some changes.

The results of the second mammogram revealed a suspicious area, and I was immediately given an ultrasound on my right breast. When the radiologist came in and told me she recommended a breast biopsy, I saw the nurse was leaning against the wall in the corner of the room. I could tell by the sympathetic look on her face that I was in trouble. I left the hospital in tears.

One week later on September 22, my wedding anniversary, I had the breast biopsy, and my husband and I drove from Atlantic City to Philadelphia to deliver the mammography slides to The Hospital of the University of Pennsylvania (UPenn). That was Friday. On Monday, our family doctor called and told my husband that the biopsy had shown that the growth was malignant. I had breast cancer. My body trembled as I absorbed the news. I fell on our bed with my knees to my chest and tried to shelter myself from what I was hearing.

The next day, I traveled with my husband to the Rena Rowan Breast Center at UPenn. We walked into the waiting room and sat. My mind was in shock. Here it was only four days after the breast biopsy, and my husband and I were meeting with the surgeon and having a conversation I could barely comprehend.

Six days later, my brother John called me. The next day, I sent an e-mail to him and ended with something I had never said to him: "I love you."

Not a Baby Sister

It was not cancer but my brother John who sent me on my first trip to the hospital. Dad had a hobby of buying old houses and then arranging the family vacation so everyone was available to fix up the disaster. We spent our vacations scraping, painting, scrubbing, and removing rubble.

We were on one such planned vacation, working on a house we affectionately had named the "white monster," when John decided to take a break and play out front. John worked very hard at avoiding hard labor. He was racing with a wagon/wheelbarrow sort of contraption on the broken-up sidewalk in front of the white monster. Being four years younger, I thought it looked like he was having fun, so I raced to the end of the wagon and attempted to jump in the moving vehicle. John yanked it, and I fell on the broken sidewalk and tore open my knee.

I was taken to the local emergency room, where the doctor sewed five stitches, and then my family returned to the white monster. I was never convinced (even with my parents' chidings) that John was genuinely concerned about my knee. His opinion was that it was stupid for me to try to jump into a moving vehicle, and that by doing so I was just asking to get hurt.

My brother John never wanted a baby sister. For three and a half years he had been the baby of the family, the last of three children born to Margaret and David Canine. Then one day, my mother told him he was going to have a baby brother or sister (there was no ultrasound back then). This was not good news for John. As he recalls:

I did not ask for a baby brother or sister. In fact, I kind of liked getting all the attention myself. My older brother and I had a great relationship, and my older sister was a teenager whom I rarely saw. I did not think we needed anyone else in the family—we were already a family of five, the "perfect" family back in the 1950s.

Nevertheless, it happened. On August 27, 1952, Rebecca Sue Canine was born. From that time on I had to yell, scream, cry, tease, perform, and in general, engage in bad behavior just to get a smidge of attention. In my mind, my mother's beautiful baby girl got it all.

Someone might think I am exaggerating or I could not possibly remember that well at that age. Pictures are proof! When I was eleven and Becky was seven, our mother took us to a small photography studio in our hometown of Blanchester, Ohio. My sister was dressed in a black and white birthday party dress with all the "fixings," plus an umbrella. Interestingly, it was not raining that day, and I think my mother called the umbrella a "parasol." I was in a shirt and tie with a sport jacket.

The photographer seemed to take hundreds of pictures. I was in very few, and hardly in any by myself. Becky was in all of them. It was pose after pose, picture after picture, smile after smile, and I thought it would never end. Everybody seemed to be excited about what was happening except me. I would have rather been playing baseball, and besides, when I heard the photographer say Becky's pictures were going to be good enough to display in the studio window, I truly lost interest.

If there ever was a defining moment in the childhood relationship I had with my younger sister, it happened a week later while I was walking home from school with some of my friends. We had to walk by the photography studio, and as we did, one of my buddies looked up to see my sister's pictures in the window. It was embarrassing enough to see her pictures there like some movie star, but even more embarrassing was the fact that I was not in any of them. Actually, as one of my friends pointed out, I was "nowhere to be seen."

My so-called friends had a lot of fun at my expense whenever we passed that studio on the way home from school. They seemed to derive a sick sort of pleasure in reminding me that my picture was not in the display window. They told me things like, "Your mom and dad like her better," "She is going to make millions of dollars being a model," and "Everybody knows who your sister is, but nobody knows you."

I finally had enough, and because I was the leader of this little band of preteen misfits, one day after school I told them we were walking home a different way. I thought that would solve the problem, but little did I know that a greater and longer-lasting issue was just beginning. My sister and I began to distance ourselves from each other.

At the beginning this was probably somewhat normal, but after a few years our relationship became characterized by competition, one-upmanship, over-achievement, and apathy. Becky competed against me through "brain power"; she was the intellectual and educationally a hard worker. I competed through athletics, working hard to be the best I could be.

As we grew older, all I really wanted was for my big brother to accept me and acknowledge that I was special. He was an all-state basketball player, a college star, and the life of the party at every family gathering. I admired him greatly, and I secretly hoped he was proud of me. I studied hard and became the valedictorian of my high school class and the President Award Recipient at the college I attended. He applauded when I received these awards, but I was never sure how sincerely.

John married in 1967, and I in 1973. Children soon followed, and for many years we lived in separate states.

Our communication revolved around family gatherings on holidays, occasional summer meetings at the river cottage, funerals, and the hospital waiting room when our dad had open-heart surgery.

John got his first doctorate in education, writing his dissertation on grief. He earned his second doctorate in psychology and had a successful counseling practice. I was a minister's wife and a teacher for nineteen years, and then I became principal of a local school. John and I stayed in contact through typical extended family experiences and Christmas cards, but at the time of my diagnosis we had not spoken to each other in two years.

Email Connection

As I mentioned, John called me eight days after I received the news of the diagnosis. I think God knew I could use a psychologist and counselor during this time and the surgeries and treatments that followed. More importantly, I think He knew I needed my brother. John was someone who could help me concentrate on life and not focus on whether I would die from the disease. He was someone who would support and encourage me throughout the treatment process. It happened through e-mails.

> *Tuesday, October 3, 2006*
> Hi, John,
> We were at the Eagles game last evening and didn't get home until one A.M. I'm exhausted, but it was good to have some fun and talk about something other than cancer.
> My receptor report was encouraging. It was not HER2/positive; it was 98 percent estrogen and 95 percent progesterone. I told Steve that I always did like to get A's.

Tuesday, I go to UPenn to participate in a testing protocol. They will complete a CAT scan, PET scan, breast MRI, and digital mammography. After the tests, I will discuss with the surgeon my surgery options. After the surgery and the node results, I'll meet with an oncologist to determine treatment options.

I have a very close friend, Sue, who is HER2/positive, and the cancer has metastasized to her lungs. She is going to UPenn, but the Herceptin and chemotherapy treatments have not worked. She just started a clinical trial program. She and her husband met Steve and me at UPenn last week when I had my first appointment. It is hard not to superimpose her experience on mine. I've had some sleepless nights.

I asked Steve, "Where is God and faith?" I have prayed for the past year for Sue, and she continues to get bad news. Now I find myself going through the same thing. I'm scared.

Through some tearful prayer times, confession, and pouring out of my heart, God has given me peace. More than anything, I want to know His presence in my life whether that is in life or death, hard times or good times. As Sue often tells me, "It is going to be OK." If she lives it is OK, and if she dies, it is really OK.

I love you,
Becky

Wednesday, October 4, 2006
Becky,

"If I find in myself a desire which no experience in this world can satisfy, the most probable explanation is that I was made for another world" (C.S. Lewis)[2]. Sometimes I am not sure where God is . . . maybe distant thunder . . . but I always come back to the fact that He wants all of me. That is where He is, waiting for full communion with me . . . which will not be completed until death. Having said that, I am fairly confident

23

that you are not going to die for a long time. All the signs thus far seem to be in your favor for a complete recovery, and I will believe by faith in that. However, you will then be left with the hard part: for what purpose did God bring this into your life? That has been the hardest question for me in my life. We are praying daily for you.

Love you,
John

You are Going to Have Time

In over five thousand communities in twenty countries, more than 500,000 cancer survivors walk in the opening lap of Relay for Life. Yes, they walk, a normal, healthy everyday activity. These people are not bound to a bed or a house. When they are walking, they are not sitting in a chair receiving chemo or laying in a hospital bed wishing they never had been diagnosed with cancer. They are out and active, with friends, celebrating life. They are living life after cancer. This year, the American Cancer Society (www.cancer.org; 1-800-ACS-2345), which sponsors the event, will help eleven million cancer survivors celebrate a birthday of surviving cancer.

Because cancer is a life-threatening illness, though, it is normal for a person receiving a new diagnosis to equate cancer with death. But the truth is many people live years with cancer, and their treatments enable them to lead normal lives. Furthermore, on a daily basis, medical science is getting closer to finding cures for many cancers. Cancer patients—especially those recently diagnosed—need to know they have time to live. Death is inevitable, of course, but cancer does not make it imminent. We are created to live. Therefore, we must embrace life.

On October 9, 2006, I underwent my first surgery to remove the cancer in my body—a lumpectomy with sentinel node biopsy. As I recovered, my brother helped me connect to life at a time when I was absorbed with death.

Monday, October 23, 2006
John,
My next biggest hurdle will be the chemo decision. I'm dreading it. I picture myself in hospice care, saying goodbye to family, lying in a hospital bed in the living room with oxygen tubes coming out of my mouth as I gasp for air. Every so often these thoughts lead me to a meltdown. I had one today, and then I decided it was time to live my life and get back to school. Spending a couple of hours at school was good therapy. Retirement is looking better all the time.

Yesterday, a missionary was with us. He told Steve that his first wife survived two mastectomies and then died in a car accident. You just never know how much time you have. Yet, I know that worrying about my days isn't going to add one more hour to my life.

Love ya,
Becky

Tuesday, October 24, 2006
Becky,
Time is a most interesting concept. None of us know how much of it we have, and it does not exist in eternity. I guess that leaves us with the issue of quality. The quality of our time is the meaningfulness of life. No matter what, in regard to your cancer, you are going to have a lot of time. Don't focus so much on the junkyard that you miss the beauty of the green grass and the blue sky. OK, I realize this is a random thought, so feel free to revise, expand, or throw it out, but in the end (sorry to use that

word) this type of thinking is the stuff of life—a process our family does well.

Love ya, and I pray for you daily,
John

One of the worst things about my big brother when we were younger was his ability to knock the breath out of me. Mother often said he did not know his own strength, and a push or a knock to the ground would leave me breathless and panicked for a moment. Cancer was the same way. It had a lot of strength and knocked the breath out of me. Now it had tightened my chest in fear, suffocating the life I so enjoyed.

Whenever I visited the oncologists, all they talked about were percentages and chances of survival. I wanted to wear a big sandwich-board sign that said "100 percent" in huge letters to remind myself that their percentages were not going to affect my story. Regardless of how much time I had left on this earth, I was going to live 100 percent of the life that God had given me.

Tuesday, October 31, 2006
John,
The tumor in the node is complicating the process. The surgeon says there is a 50 percent chance that he will find more cancer in the nodes when he does the second surgery. Also, the tumor in the node makes my survival rate lower (about 75 percent), which is why they are encouraging me to have chemo after the surgery. My percentages decrease further if they find cancer in more nodes. I finally said to my surgeon that they have percentages for everything. He smiled and said that my frustration with percentages is justified, because when you survive, then you have a 100 percent chance of survival.

It is hard to remain positive when I am faced with all these percentages. It's as if the doctors are having all of us cancer patients sit in a circle for a game of Duck, Duck, Goose, only the words they use when they tap you on the head are "live, live, live, die . . ."

I have not slept the last two nights. The fear is worse than the cancer. The spiritual struggle is worse than the physical one. Last evening, I cried and read my Bible. There were tissues all over the floor this morning. I begged God to give me some sense of peace and comfort. He did. I have no answers and I am still horrified at the thought of chemo, but God did meet my needs today.

Thank you for your thoughts and prayers.

I love you,

Becky

Tuesday, October 31, 2006

Becky,

Stay close to God. He is your protector. He will order each and every step you take. No one knows what you are going through but you and Him, and that is all that needs to be known. Please try to remain positive about this. Let them continue to evaluate and gather the information, and then sit down with your family and make some decisions. Put them into a plan of action, and then work toward the goal you desire. "Delight yourself in the Lord and he will give you the desires of your heart" (Ps. 37:4). All the while, pray for wisdom and healing, and remember that God is forever with us.

We all are praying for you, and we love you,

John

Surviving

For a long time, I did not accept the cancer diagnosis. My life had drastically changed, and there was no time to absorb the shock. It was difficult to think about surviving.

After all, how could I concentrate on surviving something I didn't want to have?

Every time I had a medical phone call or went to an appointment, they would ask for my name and my date of birth. I hated to say my name, and giving my date of birth was another slug in the stomach. Each time I gave this information, it forced me to admit I had cancer and acknowledge everything that was happening to me. This was not me. This was not the life I had planned or the future I wanted. I was young. I wanted to finish my doctorate at Rutgers, complete a few years as an administrator in our elementary school, and continue teaching in the ladies' Bible study and other ministries at church. I felt mocked every time I gave my name and date of birth. I was overwhelmed. I couldn't concentrate.

Wednesday, November 1, 2006
Becky,

I am sure your head is spinning with all the information you are receiving. You are doing the right thing; you need the information to make appropriate decisions. My next-door neighbor is an attorney/physician, and he told me about a thirty-year-old woman he knows who had breast cancer in many nodes. She went through six months of hell with radiation and chemo. It has now been two years, and she is cancer free. She works out and looks great.

He also told me some time ago about his aunt who was diagnosed with breast cancer in her fifties. She had two treatments of chemo and then told the doctors she wouldn't have any more. She lived to be seventy-five. You would need a lot more information before you make a decision like that, but the point is to not give the cancer any more power than it has by thinking negatively. The 75 percent chance of survival your doctors gave you is for you to reach your life expectancy, which is eighty years of age. We both know all the things that could happen before you reach eighty. We also know all the things that science could uncover in the next few years that will help many cancer patients (one of the few positives of capitalism).

At this point, we all need to be supporting you and encouraging you to fight this disease with all the strength God can give you. You have every right to be afraid. None of us will ever be able to understand what you are going through, but try to keep your focus on the future. That is where your hope is. How you handle the disease and treatment is up to you. Do what you need to do, but be self-protective. Keep your attention on the quality of life you believe God has for you. He does not like this disease, and He does not want you to have it. So, therefore, you must believe and have faith that He will heal you.

John

My brother helped me realize that even though cancer was a part of my life story, I needed to concentrate on living. There are millions of people who have survived various cancers. These individuals don't wear signs when they are out shopping and in public, so you never know who they are simply by sight. A few public figures, such as Lance Armstrong (a fourteen-year cancer survivor), have stepped forward to share their stories, and they are an inspiration to all suffering from the disease.

Cancer Survivors Network, an organization sponsored by the American Cancer Society, provides story after story on their website of people who have survived everything from breast cancer to prostate cancer. Some have had stage four with extreme node involvement, which makes their treatment more difficult and their chances of survival not as clear. With early detection and better treatments, many women are beating breast cancer. In fact, of all cancers, breast cancer survivors are the largest group, and detection and treatments are continuing to improve. (Actually, the number one killer of women is heart disease—it kills ten times more women every year than breast cancer.)

Although cancer had drastically altered my life, I could lead a normal life and enjoy work and time with my friends and family. I could live fully the days and time I had been given. In spite of my circumstances, I could connect to life and enjoy the blue sky and green grass.

Green Grass in the Junkyard

All it would take was for one of us kids to get a splinter or small cut on our hand and Dad would say, "The last guy I knew who had that died." We'd stop crying and laugh, because we knew kids didn't die from splinters. Dad helped us to laugh at our cuts and bruises, and afterward we felt better.

But cancer is no joke. Although I thrived on the stories of cancer survivors, I knew many people diagnosed with the disease did not survive, and I cringed each time someone told me of a friend who had died. One day after my diagnosis, I was standing in the school office when a mom came in to check out her child. I asked her about their family and how they had been. The mom proceeded to tell me that the family had recently been to a family member's funeral. I gave my sympathies and then asked about the situation. The mom looked at me with fear and said, "I can't tell you." Then she literally ran out of the office without her child. I turned to the secretary and with a smile knowingly said, "She must have died from breast cancer."

As my brother said, cancer is a junkyard. Yet, he had also advised me not to focus so much on the junkyard that I missed the blue sky and green grass. Each day God had something He intended for me to enjoy. As long as I had life, I had hope. I was probably not going to die tomorrow, so I needed to live today. People survive cancer, car accidents, heart attacks, and other tragedies. I had to concentrate on the survivors, life, blue skies, and green grass.

On mornings when I was paralyzed with fear, I simply said, "I'm probably not going to die today, so get up and live." This day, this moment, is all that we have, and we need to live 100 percent of the life that God has given us. Nothing, not even a cancer diagnosis, should make us miss the blue sky and the green grass.

Wednesday, November 1, 2006
John,
Thanks for the prayers. There are times when I cry and pour out my heart to God and He gives me such a sense of peace, but there are times when it is difficult to pray. During such times when I am spiritually weak, I know the prayers of others are carrying me through.

There was cancer in the nodes. One, the sentinel node, had a tumor. This has been the biggest test of faith I have faced in my life. I want to know God's presence, and I don't want fear or anything to separate me from God's love. But I am scared.

I do believe God will heal me, yet I cannot presume. As I told you, one of my best friends has breast cancer that has gone to her lungs. She is in a clinical trial program at UPenn. Before I knew I had cancer, I had cried and prayed with her on many occasions. It is hard to set her experience aside and realize I am a different person with a different cancer.

On a lighter topic, I had a third-grade student yesterday who was sent to my office for calling his teacher a bad name. I would tell you the word he used, but your e-mail filter would probably block it . . . let's just say it was really offensive. The funny part is I didn't know what

31

the word meant, so I had to have the student sit in the hall while I called Steve to ask him. Fortunately, after talking with the boy, I was sure he didn't know what the word meant either. He just knew it wasn't nice. I'll spare you the rest of the details.
Love ya,
Becky

Thursday, November 2, 2006
Becky,
Your e-mail gave me a good laugh . . . you ought to hear some of the words out of our six-year-old Sophia's mouth. She has no idea what they mean. One time when she and Nanci were out trick-or-treating on Halloween, she said she was "pissed off" that it was so cold.

Anyway, take your time with all this and be involved in all the decisions that are made. I believe the Spirit does approach God on our behalf when we are too tired, afraid, or angry to pray, and I believe the prayers of others accomplish much. Friday night and all day Saturday, I teach a death and dying graduate class at Spring Arbor (hopefully you'll find some humor in that). I am convinced that you are going to live a lot longer than you think, and I am not convinced that you will die of cancer. However, I am convinced we both will die some day . . .we are terminal.
Enjoy today. Love ya,
John

Thursday, November 2, 2006
John,
I don't know how I would walk through this without your support. God must have known that someday I'd need an older brother who was a counselor. My reconnection to you has been worth the cancer. OK, so the "worth" it is an exaggeration, but your confidence helps me be positive.

CONNECT TO LIFE

My next surgery is scheduled for November 9. My verse for the day is Isaiah 41:10. I have said it so many times that I have it memorized. Let's see if I can type it: "So do not fear, for I am with you; do not be dismayed, for I am your God. I will strengthen you and help you; I will uphold you with my righteous right hand." Interestingly, that was one of Dad's favorite verses. After today, I know why. It was my anchor all day. At one point as I was walking the school halls, I told God, "I understand why You gave Yourself as God to people; I can't make it through this without You. I need You with me." That is backward theology, as He created us, but it makes sense for me to think of Him as my gift today. And Jesus is the gift of God.

Love ya,
Becky

Friday, November 3, 2006
Becky,
Thank you for the verse—Isaiah 41:10—and especially for the thought of Dad. There are so many little things he said to me (and I'm sure to you too) that have stayed with me. Interestingly, they were not things he said in the pulpit but in private. I can honestly say there are times when I miss him and would like to see him and talk with him.

Your e-mails are showing to me a deep fellowship with a loving God. I could be wrong about this, but I believe this is what God wants from all of us and, respectfully, I say He does not care how He gets it. He will use accidents, illness, broken relationships, or any other experience to bring us closer to Him. I pray daily that He will be real in my life . . . a dangerous prayer, in my opinion, because I may not like the circumstances of His realness. Nevertheless, I need to pray it, because what He gives me is all I have.

33

I am sure we both are glad we had a father who preached the life-changing message that God came to be with us in Jesus Christ, and that Christ died for us so death would not have any sting. It takes faith to believe that.

Take care. We all love you.

John

When the nurse was preparing me for my first surgery, I told him I never expected to have cancer. I was always going to have heart disease. After all, my dad had died of heart disease, and I had many relatives who had died from heart problems. The nurse's answer to me was, "Well, we'll get you all fixed up with this, and that can still happen." He was making the same point John had made—that I was going to live a lot longer than I thought right then, and that he wasn't convinced that I would die of cancer. So whatever the junkyard of life deals you, play your hand, connect to life, and cherish the blue sky and green grass.

Chapter 2

Enjoy Hugs and Home

*When you touch someone, you know they are. Hugs are
good, they feel nice, and if you don't believe it, try it.*[1]
—Leo Buscaglia

Hugs Build Bridges

IT WAS EIGHT months later, during an extended family
reunion on July 4, 2007, that I saw my brother for the
first time after my diagnosis and treatments. Even with
the e-mails we had been sending to each other, I wasn't sure
what I would do when I saw him in person. I was afraid
the moment would be awkward. My sister was planning
the reunion, and I was to be the honored guest. We were
celebrating the end of my cancer treatments. I had only a
little fuzz on my head, so I wore a scarf.

My brother, Nanci, Steve, and I would be staying at the
local Holiday Inn. After Steve and I arrived and checked
into our room, we went to the front lobby and asked them
to call my brother's room to let him know we were there. I

hadn't seen John in two years, but when he and Nanci came to the lobby, he still looked the same to me. I, on the other hand, looked much different—I was thin and bald because of the cancer treatments.

John had a package for me. In it was a silver picture frame with one of his sayings etched on it: "Overcoming life's challenges creates eternal joy." I had a gift for him as well: a word plaque for his desk that simply said, "HOPE." John and I told each other later that we had thought the gifts would be appropriate messages and serve as significant memoirs, but it was really the hug we shared when we met that we will both remember. It eased the awkwardness of the moment. Hugs build bridges and heal spiritual, emotional, and even physical hurts.

It's Never Too Late to Hug

When I was growing up, my father was never one to give hugs to his sons. He joked, teased, praised, and supported them in every way, but he was not one to physically reach out with hugs. As John recalls:

> This might be hard to understand, but my father never hugged me until the last year of his life. Why? I am not sure. I expect it was because of the fact that he was a man's man. He was raised on a farm in Indiana, walked five miles to school every day (after he had milked ten cows—I heard that story often), and had boxing matches at the county fair. He simply did not believe in hugging other men. In place of hugging, he always shook my hand. Whenever I would leave home, and when I would return, it was always the same—a handshake.
>
> During the winter of his seventieth year, I took my family to visit my parents in Lake Worth, Florida. My father had semi-retired, and he and my mother traveled

between their two homes in Indiana and Florida. We spent seven wonderful days in sunshine and eighty-degree temperatures. We went deep-sea fishing; played football on the beach; ate oranges, grapefruit and tangerines; went to the early-bird special dinner each night; and played games in the evening. My three sons loved it.

When we arrived, I gave my father a copy of Leo Buscaglia's book *Loving Each Other*. In the book, Buscaglia discusses how each of us needs at least four hugs each day, and that when we learn to hug each other, we learn to build bridges rather than walls. Hugs make us feel better and, most importantly, they send a message to others that we love and care about them. My father read the book from cover to cover.

When it came time to leave Florida, none of us wanted to go. After we had packed and taken a last look around to make sure we hadn't forgotten anything, we got in line to say goodbye. My mother started with her strong, lingering, kissy German hugs. I am not sure the boys ever developed an appreciation for their grandmother's hugs, but they endured waiting for their grandpa's handshake. However, this time we all were fooled.

When it was my father's turn to say goodbye, he pushed my oldest son's hand away and gave him a big hug. He did the same with sons number 2 and 3. When he approached me, I thought he surely would not hug me, but he did. It felt so good, so right, and so warm and genuine. I realized this was something I had missed and wanted more of. And then, three months later, he died.

I could regret what I did not get. However, I choose to remember what I always will have: a wonderful gift from a teachable father who was not afraid to learn and change, even at the end of his life. The memory of my father's hug has been quite healing for many of my human hurts.

In the same way that John will remember Dad's hug, I will remember the first real hug I had from my brother in the lobby of the Holiday Inn. With the hug, he seemed to be saying, "I acknowledge you as special in my life. I know you are there, and I care about what happens to you."

Peace of God

Even with the hugs, I still struggled with finding peace in this situation. Most days I reacted like a deer caught in the headlights. I had watched Dad when he had congestive heart failure. After one of his episodes in which he almost died, Dad told me he had met his last enemy, death. I wondered at the time what he meant. Now I was facing the same enemy, and I was more scared than I ever thought I would be. All my life I had heard about God's peace, but some days it wasn't there.

Saturday, November 4, 2006
John,
Thank God for Dad. I have thought of him often as I have gone through this process. He had struggles just like we have, but he was so authentic in his relationship with God.
I had a precious time with God this morning. I was reflecting on Psalm 119:76-77: "May your unfailing love be my comfort, according to your promise to your servant. Let your compassion come to me that I may live, for your law is my delight." Since September 14, I've been struggling with peace. I've functioned and gone forward, but life has been hard. I think I would rather not live than to go through life without the assurance of His peace and presence. I need a permanent peace that is unexplainable, but that calms the heart.

I felt as I prayed this morning that God is going to heal me. I don't want to be presumptuous, and I don't want to depart from the peace that He has given me in surrendering to Him. I am praying for Him to take control of the situation and bring healing. Today in my journal I wrote, "God, please, if I might ask, when it is my time to pass from this life and come to be with You, may it be a gracious transition—one that is filled with Your love and peace. When I do travel from here to be with You for all eternity, I want it to be a trip like none other—filled with grace and peace, not fear and dismay. Thank You, God. I believe that You will answer this request."

John, one time a few years back, I remember you using a rubber band illustration in reference to grief. I believe it had to do with people feeling tense after the loss of a loved one. I have felt like that rubber band—stretched, and thinking that I might snap. But God has been gracious and, in the worst of it, has kept me from snapping. I want to live in His peace.

I love you,
Becky

Tuesday, November 7, 2006
Becky

I am getting ready to leave the office and read your e-mails again. I believe I know what God's peace is. I do not always have it, but that is probably the reason I know what it is—and the reason that when I get it, it is so good. There is a difference between happiness and God's peace. Happiness is the sun coming through the clouds on an overcast day, but God's peace is a sense of satisfaction and contentment, whether it's sunny or cloudy. When we strive for happiness, we are under a delusion and will never have God's peace. God's peace is much richer and deeper.

I really believe God will give us "dying grace" when we leave this earth—death that happens with satisfaction

39

and dignity. I often wonder about the healing part. We have been spiritually healed, but is that all we need? Should we pray for healing for everything from colds to cancer? However, I have come to the conclusion that God wants to hear from us and is concerned about our wellbeing, so I believe prayers for healing are appropriate. My prayer has been for God to take away the cancer from your body.

I will be praying hard for your second surgery on Thursday. I trust they will find no more positive nodes. If all of your body scans come back normal, I think you will be fine. You will have to make some decisions about treatment. I do relate to your thoughts that all this is in God's hands and He will do with my little sister what He wants, because she belongs to Him. I believe He wants to heal you, and I will continue to pray that way.

Love you,
John

Tuesday, November 7, 2006
John,
Psalm 119 has been an encouragement. The writer asks many times for God to preserve his life according to God's love, law, and righteousness. I'm praying God will take all the cancer from me, yet even in that prayer, I am more aware of the awesome responsibility it brings. If God heals me and gives me many more years, I want to live differently and be more in love with Him. I want to know His presence and extend my worship to Him. I hope I never go back to getting worked up over some of the things that have upset me in the past. Today I thought, *I wonder how God feels when He prepares a home in heaven for us and we panic and worry about going there?* It doesn't make sense. Thanks for being there.

I love you,
Becky

Wednesday, November 8, 2006
Becky,
If we were able to take a weekend vacation and check in our heavenly home, I doubt we would ever check out. But we are so human. If it is not too much trouble, please have Steve call me after your surgery. It sounds to me like you are doing all you can. Keep your focus, and remember . . . it is never as good as it sounds or as bad as it seems.
Love you,
John

Home

Growing up, our family lived in an old white clapboard parsonage with a sinking back porch. It had a big dining room and living room and three bedrooms upstairs. It wasn't elaborate or fancy; in fact, if it wasn't situated in our small town, you simply might have called it a country home. The backyard offered a croquet court, sandbox, and garden. We never had a cat, so mice often greeted us in the morning. You had to be cautious in the downstairs hall. It was always a good idea to peek around the corner before you set foot in the hallway, or otherwise you might have to jump to avoid a furry critter.

Although we called this place home, what really defined it were the experiences, conversations, love, and laughter we shared there. We frequently entertained missionaries, visiting pastors, evangelists, and family friends. Croquet was a part of the summer evening schedule, and games of Rook occupied our time on the cooler evenings or holidays. Everyone in the family played a part. As the little sister, I shagged the croquet balls, an important job to the continuance of the game. We listened to each other's stories and laughed at Dad's jokes.

The house on 306 West Center Street isn't there anymore. The church needed space for a parking lot, and it was torn down. Yet my mind still "sees" that house, and I know it is home.

We don't know much about the heavenly home we will have after we breathe our last here on earth. The Bible is strangely silent on the subject. Yet even though we may not be able to describe our "home" after this life, we can know it will be about experiences, conversations, love, and laughter. It will be about the people, and mostly about the presence of Jesus. The Bible says that to be absent from the body is to be present with the Lord.

As my brother said, if we took a weekend vacation and checked in our heavenly home, I doubt we would ever check out. I know I have not checked out of my earthly home (I'm not ready just yet), but I also know by faith that my destiny is my heavenly home—my true haven. And I am sure it will be something beyond my imagination.

Second Surgery

On November 9, 2006, I underwent my second cancer surgery: an axillary node dissection to remove twenty-six nodes and examine them for evidence of cancer. A drain was placed under my arm, and I spent the night in the hospital. Five days later, I wrote back to John to tell him how the surgery had gone.

Tuesday, November 14, 2006
John,
I think I am in denial, but I will come out of it quickly tomorrow when I meet with the oncologist. I have not heard anything from the surgery pathology report and probably won't until tomorrow. I have a drain under my arm. It's painful to read anything about cancer and

treatments. I'm tired and weak from surgery, and my friend Sue is not doing well.

The night in the hospital, with a little help from a different anesthesia, was one of prayer. The lady next to me was in a lot of pain, and she asked me to pray for her. We prayed together. One of the nurses knew I was praying and asked me to pray for her, too. I was awake most of the evening, as the emergency helicopter landed right outside my window. I prayed each time I heard it. It was exhausting.

Overall, when I am not thinking about my friend Sue, I am in good spirits and have a peace that God is going to heal me. Yet, Sue is a constant reminder that I cannot presume anything. Meanwhile, I am left with what you said in an earlier e-mail: for what purpose did God bring this into my life, and for what purpose has He spared me? I never want to question His love and His shepherding of my life.

Home is a haven from the storms; a good place to rest.

Love ya,
Becky

Chapter 3

. . . .

ACCEPT THE CHALLENGE

Time flies when you're having fun, but a week seems like a month when life goes sour. Sometimes it is not the severity of the trial but the continuance of it that wears us down and causes us to sink into despondency. Our question turns from "Why?" to "How long?" Remember, God has not forgotten you in your trial. He will give you the strength you need to handle whatever comes.
(Source unknown – words from a card sent by a friend)

First Visit with the Oncologist

STEVE AND I were ushered into a small examination room on the fourteenth floor of Penn Towers, the Rena Rowan Breast Center. We could see Philadelphia and the stadium where our son Joshua had run in the Penn relays twelve years previous. On that day, like this day, it was the results that we so anxiously awaited.

I held my brown notebook ready to record what the doctor told us. After a few minutes, he walked in with his fellow doctor. His comments were quick and direct. It went something like this: "If the cancer comes back to the breast, you will need to have a mastectomy. However, it can metastasize to your lungs, liver, bones, or brain. If it does that, you are terminal." I sat there thinking, *All right, you could have started on a bit more positive note or given me some encouragement.* He talked about the tumors in the nodes, chemo regimens, percentages, and how I would have even better chances if I had chemo. He then said they were leaving to discuss my case. I think he did that to give my husband and me some time to absorb the information.

Two days later, I wrote to John and told him about the visit:

Friday, November 17, 2006
John,
We met with the oncologist on Wednesday. They are serious people. It takes a couple of days to process the information and adjust to the news. They tested twenty-six more nodes, and only one was positive. That node did not have a tumor, just a trace. That puts my node involvement at three, which is considered a better scenario. However, they say that any node involvement is serious.

The oncologist said they are going to consider the cancer as having been surgically removed. They don't know what else might be going on, so they don't want to treat things they don't know for sure are there. He agreed with me when I said that out of a hundred women in my situation, ninety would receive chemo unnecessarily. However, he added that chemo and radiation and Tomoxifin would increase my survival rate from 80 percent to 90 percent, or even better.

The chemo the doctor is recommending is Taxotere/ Cytoxan. It does not cause heart damage or much nausea.

I will lose my hair and experience the other common side effects that are associated with other chemos. It will be four treatments, every three weeks. He says all the bad side effects can be rebuilt after treatment and that the only permanent damage may be to my ovaries, which is not a bad thing as they are the most common producers of estrogen. He agreed that treatment for people like me may look very different in thirty years.

I will probably start chemo the first Wednesday in December. I should begin losing my hair on December 24. I can treat losing my hair as an adventure—I think. My biggest prayer is that the cancer is not anywhere else and that God will remove any chance of it returning.

My friend Sue was back at UPenn today and was coughing up blood this morning. My heart aches for their family. I talked with her daughter. She is struggling with accepting the fact that this might be their last Christmas with their mom. She is hurting. I don't need an oncologist to tell me what might happen. I am seeing it firsthand.

I love you,
Becky

Monday, November 20, 2006
Becky,

Take your time in making decisions. Only you and God can make them, and time and God are on your side. I would press the doctor to give some information about cancers like yours that he has seen before—and what the outcome was. Did the node that had the tumor have any significance? How about the original cancer being less than two centimeters in size? Isn't that good? If there should be more cancer in your system, will the chemo get rid of it for sure? Maybe I ask too many questions, but I would try to get answers, or at least opinions. The information period will be over soon, if it is not already. Hang in there. I truly believe that God has a lot more for you to do, and without question our lives are in His hands.

Love you,

John

God Is on Our Side

As John explained, when we accept the challenge, we know God is on our side. Why? Simply because He created us and is committed to us. We are made in His image and created in "perfected essence." It is only when we choose to oppose God that we fall from His favor and need to be restored. Restoration—or, if you will, man's salvation—is in Jesus, who is God in man form. Jesus became the sacrifice for all of our wrongfulness. In fact, He took everything wrong from man, woman, and child, put it on Himself, and took it with Him to death. However, He came back from death to reveal eternal life in what we call heaven—which is probably more of a person (Jesus) than it is a place (heaven). Jesus is and was the ultimate love sacrifice.

It's a pretty remarkable story! On the other hand, it is not a story that can be submitted to a scientific method of inquiry. No one but Jesus has come back from the dead and visited with us. Modern science says Jesus' resurrection either didn't happen or it has no meaning. It cannot be validated, or, as John Dewey would say, there's "no warranted assertibilities here."

So how do we get God on our side? He is already there, and our awareness of this fact is increased by our personal faith in Jesus. Faith is the great connector to God and His eternal world. We believe in the story of Jesus by faith. The more we believe and have faith in Jesus and His teachings, the more God puts meaning into the circumstances of life. The more God is in our lives, the more good we can accomplish. Of course, good is not always what we think it is, but what God wants. "In all things God works for the good of those who love him" (Rom. 8:28). The same faith that connects us to God and restores us to intimacy with Him is the same faith that will bring definition to our lives. As we learn to rely on God, we are able to sense His power when we are dealing with life's issues. To this extent, faith is like a muscle in that the more you exercise it, the bigger and stronger it grows. Make no mistake: even with a life-threatening illness, God is on our side. He does not like the disease or illness. It does not come from Him, but the lesson is clear to those who believe the Jesus story: it is all about faith. Solid faith . . . growing faith . . . faith in light . . . faith in darkness . . . faith in the shadow of death . . . faith that will move mountains. Whether we live or die, we have faith. Faith is why God is on our side.

A Sense of Sudden Loss

A sense of loss can come on suddenly, and when it occurs the person who is experiencing it needs special understanding. Such losses can contribute to feelings that reality is distorted, exacerbate feelings of guilt (often expressed by "if only" statements), compel the person to blame others, instill in him or her a feeling of hopelessness (which often leaves the person paralyzed), and give a sense that there is unfinished business, which produces anger.

Throughout my diagnosis and surgeries, it was hard for me to come to grips with reality. Two of our grandchildren, aged two and four, lived within five miles of us, and to them life continued on as normal. One evening, Steve and I went to see a movie with the kids and grandkids. This simple, enjoyable activity was almost more than I could handle. I was uneasy and on edge. We went to dinner at Outback Steakhouse, and I had trouble ordering and difficulty staying sane until the food came. Eating was a fog. We went to a movie, but I couldn't concentrate. The story seemed senseless, and I couldn't figure out why I was there. Of course, it didn't make sense to be anywhere. That made every activity a chore. I sat in my chair and pretended to watch the movie, and then hugged the grandkids good night when it was over. No one knew the emotional struggles I was experiencing. Life went on, but I was a distant bystander.

It took a while for me to understand what was going on, but eventually it dawned on me that I was experiencing loss. I wrote to John a few days later to tell him about what I had discovered.

Monday, November 20, 2006
John,
You were so right about accepting the situation and moving forward. I went back to school today for the first full day since the second surgery. I suddenly realize what bothers me: among other things, there is a tremendous sense of sudden loss. My life has drastically changed since this diagnosis. I'm sure it is not like the loss of a child or mate, but nonetheless there is grief, and accepting it and learning to live with this as my new normal is part of the process. I know God is in control of my life, and I am open to His working in my life. This could be an exciting adventure.

I got the results back from the trans-vaginal exam that I had before the second surgery. My uterus is thickened and there are two cysts, one on each ovary. Based on the radiology report, the doctors are recommending that I have another trans-vaginal exam. My gynecologist called this evening and scheduled me for a biopsy of the uterus

on Wednesday. He doesn't suspect anything, but he wants to be sure before I go into chemo and begin Tamoxifin. Happy Thanksgiving!
Love ya,
Becky

Tuesday, November 21, 2006
Becky,
I would assume you need a break from all of this. Please take it. Recharge yourself the next few days and only talk about it when you need to or want to. Remember, in this life we are not going to live forever, but we are probably not going to die soon. So don't miss the enjoyment each day can bring. I have enjoyed our e-mails and hope we can continue. I will be gone the next three weeks, and I do not have a laptop or the ability to check my e-mails. But please update me when you feel like it. You have a lot of purpose left, and you must believe that.
Love you and pray for you daily.
John

November Diagnosis

It was about seven P.M. on Tuesday, November 28, a week after John's last e-mail. Steve and I were driving back from UPenn, where the doctors had checked my drain from the second surgery. It had been two months and four days since I had first been diagnosed with breast cancer. It was a quiet ride home. I usually sat and stared on trips home from UPenn. There was always so much to absorb.

Suddenly, Steve's cell phone rang. It was Jodie, our third child who still lived at home. The gynecologist had called the house asking for Steve. She thought that was odd, so she called to tell us. Steve and I discussed what this could mean. Had we not paid a bill, or was there a problem with the insurance company regarding one of the tests? I couldn't have cared less about the financial end; I was struggling with the emotions.

Then the cell phone rang again. This time it was my gynecologist. Steve took the phone call, and I could tell by the "oh," "OK," "well," and "um," that the conversation was not going well. How much money could we possibly owe? Steve closed his phone and said, "Your uterine biopsy was positive. There seems to be some confusion as to whether it is metastasized breast cancer or a new cancer."

If the first cancer diagnosis had scared me, this second diagnosis within two months absolutely destroyed me. I didn't cry. I didn't talk. I was paralyzed. After several minutes, I figured the best person to know this news was my oncologist at UPenn. I knew he was there, as I had just left. So I took Steve's cell phone and called. I reached his nurse and explained this new development to her. She said, "Just a minute," and immediately Dr. Fox was on the phone.

Dr. Fox's first words after I explained the situation to him were, "Oh, no." I knew I was in trouble. Oncologists are too calculated and composed to say "oh, no." I gave him my gynecologist's number, and he gave me his beeper number. The doctors and lab technicians would talk the next day and determine the nature of the second cancer. Steve and I headed home to share the news with my mom and our children. Neither of us spoke. We just drove.

We pulled into the driveway and I exited the car. I was sure I was no taller than two feet high, and I wasn't sure I could make it up the steps that led to our house. I don't remember who told Mom and our two daughters. I just remember there was silence, and then tears. I was the mom, the orchestrator of encouragement, but I had nothing positive to say. I couldn't fake it, so I retreated to the bedroom to cry.

I should not have slept that night, but God gave me a miracle. All night, He held me above the mattress. Now I'm sure that if you had asked Steve, he would have told you I was right beside him, but I wasn't. I slept well, but the few times I did wake, I knew God's hand was lifting me up. In fact, I wondered each time why Steve wasn't sleeping up where I was. I was having a peaceful time in God's hand, and there Steve was down on the bed. Hadn't God said, "So do not fear, for I am with you; do not be dismayed, for I am your God. I will strengthen you and help you; I will uphold you with my righteous right hand" (Isa. 41:10)?

Wednesday, November 29, 2006
Dear John,
   I don't know how long it will take you to get this message, but thought I better give you an update. My gynecologist called last night, and my biopsy showed that I have uterine cancer. It has been a long day of phone calls and discussion, but I will see a gynecological oncologist the first part of next week and then have another surgery. My oncologist at UPenn is working to get me on a fast track for surgery. Chemo will be put on hold until after this next surgery. I am shocked and stunned. They did some further tests on the sample and are sure that this cancer is not from the breast. It is a separate cancer. That is good.
   Although I am overwhelmed, God has given me peace. I believe God enabled them to find this cancer because He does plan to heal me. My gynecologist and the surgeon at UPenn didn't think this biopsy was necessary; both assured me it was just a precaution and that my local gynecologist would not find anything. My ultrasound report also did not indicate that I needed this biopsy—it just indicated I should have another ultrasound in three to four months. I know God is in control of everything, and I know for sure His hand was in the discovery of this

cancer. The gynecologist said it was "fortuitous" they discovered this cancer. The dictionary says that means to happen by chance. I don't believe that; I know God's hand is in it. I hope He plans to heal me, but if not, I know He is God, good and almighty.

Please continue to pray that I will be able to mentally and physically handle another surgery. People have told me that this surgery puts you into clinical menopause and is a shock to the body.

Love ya,
Becky

Third Surgery

From the second diagnosis to the third surgery on December 12, 2006—a hysterectomy/bilateral salpingo-oophorectomy with staging and node sampling—the e-mail communication between John and me was quiet. John was upset about the second cancer and didn't respond. When he did, it was very brief.

Thursday, December 14, 2006
Becky,
No hurry, but when you get a chance give me an update. Do not be afraid to rest.
John

Chapter 4

. . . .

FIGHT THE FIGHT

Do what you can, with what you have, where you are.[1]

—Theodore Roosevelt

Fight Mode

OUR MOTHER IS of German descent. She is tough. Today, at age ninety, she is no longer as intimidating to people—she can say and do what she wants, and everyone thinks she is "cute" or "wise"—but in her younger days she was affectionately known as "Sergeant." She gave us kids an adequate amount of freedom, but when things were out of hand (or headed that way), she took control. Loud voices, excessive talk, debating, and playing to win were the norm in our house. We never were taught, "It doesn't matter if you win or lose, but how you play the game"; no, we were taught to play to win. If you lose, you try harder the next time, but you always play to win.

Before Steve and I were married, he was at our house for an evening during Christmas vacation. At one point, my two brothers, Dad, and Steve decided to play Risk. This was a big deal, because in Risk you get to build armies and rule the world. Well, Steve didn't do so well in the game, and eventually he realized there was nothing else he could do to win. Since it was late, he decided to release his armies to my brother John instead of rolling all the times necessary to be officially wiped out.

My other brother, Sam, immediately determined that this action was unacceptable and proceeded to prevent it. As my poor husband watched, my two brothers stood nose-to-nose, yelling, arguing, and gesturing. They did everything short of swearing and coming to blows (Mother did not allow those behaviors) to control the circumstances so they could win. Finally, my mother stepped in and Steve was able to release his armies to John, but my two brothers argued about it for the rest of the Christmas vacation. To this day, more than thirty years later, you could still spark a lively discussion if you were to ask either of my brothers what someone should do when exiting a Risk game prematurely.

No game was ever "just a game." We were raised to put everything we had into whatever we were doing. This was a life skill that would help me during the next few months.

Friday, December 22, 2006
Becky,
I have a few questions for you, but don't read this if you are not ready. If you are ready, then take a deep breath and focus. It is not as bad as it might seem.
The questions I would like to ask are, first, what kind of cancer is it in the pelvic nodes? I assume it is not related to the breast cancer. Second question: What kind of treatment will you have, and will the treatment

fight both kinds of cancer? Finally, since you have no female organs and your cancers are fed by estrogen, isn't it logical that the cancer at the very least would not be as aggressive? This would be of great benefit. It is like a car that has no gas; it cannot travel.

Once your body has healed to the point of starting treatment, we need to all pray that you will go into "fight mode." As Paul says in 1 Timothy 6:12, "Fight the good fight of the faith." I realize I have taken this verse out of context, but it still applies. This is about you and God and faith, and no one else can understand.

We all want you to fight hard to achieve full health. I believe this will happen. If it does not happen, I will be angry, but no matter how hard it may be, I will work at accepting God's will in your situation and in the situations of anyone else I love. I know I have said this before, but you are not dead. But if you worry about dying you will be dead, because you are going to miss life and living.

Try to enjoy the holiday season.

John

Thursday, January 4, 2007
John,

Well, another day at UPenn . . . this time to meet with the surgeon about putting in a port for chemo. We go to Fox Chase this coming Tuesday for a second opinion. The surgeon today had trouble getting my history straight and wasn't sure why I was having chemo that required a port. He was surprised that I had three surgeries in such a short time. He finally shook his head and said, "Man, what have you got, bad genes?"

We picked up my surgery report from UPenn to take to Fox Chase. I can't bring myself to read it. Steve did. It indicates that my cancer is very aggressive.

On the mental side: Your words about acceptance are so true. I sat down Tuesday evening and wrote on the calendar everything that has happened since September 14, when

I had my ultrasound and the doctor told me there was a lump in my breast. I only put down the high stress days—you know, the days I got bad news or was thrown another curve ball. I counted the days I spent in the hospital, but not the days I spent for recuperation. When I totaled it, I discovered I have had 110 high stress days from that first day in September to the end of the year. Out of those days, I had frightening situations on thirty-two days, which is 29 percent of the time.

Of course, you don't process frightening situations immediately, so there went a few more days, and then there were the days after the last two surgeries that I wasn't very mobile. After the hysterectomy, I was flat on my back for about two weeks, only doing a little walking. Also, since the surgeries, I have been thrown into surgical menopause. I haven't slept more than two to three hours at a time—I wake up in a pool of sweat, shed the bed covers, and reach for water. So as I reflect, I don't think I've had time to come to acceptance. In fact, I'm not sure I have absorbed much at all yet. My emotions are like a soggy sponge.

However, your e-mails and cards and the phone calls I have received from friends have helped me through the process. You have said, "Don't look at the junkyard and miss the beauty of the green grass and the blue sky." These thoughts are beginning to make sense to me.

Lately, my thoughts have been fear-invested and morbid. Even when I read my Bible, I'm not sure if I should repent of some specific sin, beg God for life, accept His will, rejoice in the trial, learn from the discipline, or do some combination of all these responses. I find myself feeling guilty because I am so plagued with fear and dismay that this is all happening.

Steve brought me a quote from Charles Spurgeon today that read, "It is remarkable, my Brothers and Sisters, that the Holy Spirit has given us very few deathbed scenes in the book of God. We have very few in the Old

Testament, fewer still in the New. I take it that the reason may be because the Holy Ghost would have us take more account of how we live than how we die, for life is the main business. He who learns to die daily while he lives will find it no difficulty to breathe out his soul for the last time into the hands of his faithful Creator."[2]

So tonight, I am going to bed and think about the living that God has for me tomorrow.

I love you, big brother,

Becky

Friday, January 5, 2007
Becky,

I am back in the office today. I read your email. The Spurgeon quote got to me. I cried a little—not a good way to start the day with tears on the desk! So I wiped the tears away and watched the YouTube video that you sent of the little old lady hitting a Mercedes. I laughed hard. I now have experienced the full range of human emotions and am ready to go home. Who wants to work anyway? It is fifty degrees in Detroit, and I am wondering why I went to Florida and put the boat up. I could be waterskiing right now.

Your review of the good days/bad days you have had since this started was awesome. It will hold you accountable to being as positive as possible. Just know that there is no sin in your life that has not already been forgiven. You have life right now. God's will is revealed to us as we live by faith, trials do perfect us to the image we want (Christ), and the things you have already learned are God's gifts to you. You will continue to see things that none of us will see . . . so enjoy them and be confident in that fact.

Let me know what the second opinion says.

Love you,

John

Part of the Fight Is Acceptance

When I was first diagnosed with cancer, John told me that as a part of the fight I needed to accept what was happening to me. His words sounded like good advice at the time, but they really made no sense. I did not want to accept something as life-changing as cancer. Frankly, I liked my life the way it was before cancer. I was more than willing to accept some things—gifts at Christmas, hard work, even discouraging news (that could be worked through)—but cancer? Never. So I shrugged off his advice as words from a counselor who did not actually know what I was experiencing. Yet, I kept toying with the idea of acceptance. How would it look? What did it mean?

Tuesday, January 9, 2007
John,
We went to Fox Chase today for a second opinion. This is basically what we learned:
  • The uterine cancer is now the issue. No one seems too concerned about the breast cancer anymore.
  • The uterine cancer is stage 3, but it is also grade 3, which is a very aggressive form.
  • The doctors are concerned because the cancer is already halfway through the wall of the uterus, in two nodes, and in the cervix.
  • However, the cancer is on the inside of the cervix, not the outside, which is good.
  • A Pap test would not have found it.
  • Again, the doctors confirmed that I am very fortunate the cancer was found. Whenever I tell people about it, they just look at me blankly and say, "How did they find this?" I just have to say, "God." I had none of the typical signs of uterine cancer.
  • The chemo regimen for this type of cancer is pretty much what UPenn recommends, although that is

60

why we went to Fox Chase—for them to give their final recommendation.

• All agree that the chemo will be rough, but that it would be risky not to have it. The risk of not having chemo with this type of cancer is much higher than not having it with the breast cancer. Interestingly, the chemo the doctors were recommending for the breast cancer would have been much easier on me—I could have worked full-time. However, that chemo would not have touched the uterine cancer. When they tell me information like this, I have to praise God that they found the uterine cancer. It makes me hopeful that it is because He is going to give me more days.

• The chemo can be done locally, so we don't have to take the long drives to UPenn.

• The radiation treatment for this cancer sounds brutal. All have agreed that even after three rounds of chemo, having the radiation will be in some ways as bad as the chemo. I meet with a radiologist tomorrow to discuss this further.

• The oncologist at Fox Chase strongly recommends that I have genetic testing.

I go to UPenn for a MUGA scan (this will determine if my heart is OK to receive Adriamyacen) and a CAT scan of the pelvic area on Friday. On Monday, I am supposed to go back to UPenn to have a port put in and meet with the oncologist. Then I will have to make the final decisions regarding the treatment plan. It looks as though I may start chemo on January 22 at our local hospital, Southern Ocean County Hospital.

Emotionally, there are times when I praise the Lord for revealing the uterine cancer, and then there are times when I try to politely ask Him why I had to have it at all. The awful days of 24/7 fear are gone, which is a relief, but I do still have moments of despair and discouragement. Most of this is probably due to how drastically my life has changed and the tremendous sense of loss I feel in regard to my personal and professional life. I have always been one who was driven to achieve—you know that feeling; it is somehow ingrained in us. Now, most days, I think that if I can walk my two to four miles and get my own meals, I am doing well. Thanks for being there on the other end. It is very therapeutic to write to you.

I love you!

Becky

Wednesday, January 10, 2007
Becky,

Thanks for the update. It was good to hear that the fear is not the issue it has been.

I have been so angry about the uterine cancer that I am not sure at times if I should be e-mailing you . . . please take that only as a confession of my earthly weaknesses. I keep trying to leave the situation with God, but then I find I take it back . . . I will keep working on doing the right thing (which is to believe by faith in your healing). I am sure God is humored by the fact that I am mentioning my little sister's name to Him so many times each day. He is probably saying, "What about all those other years?"

I am not sure how you can be dealing with all this—it must be that the peace of God passes all understanding. Nevertheless, if you haven't already, please go on WebMD.com and look up uterine cancer . . . the article I read was pretty good, and even though your cancer is aggressive, it is really all about how your body in general responds to the treatment. We need to pray that it does not spread to the liver, lungs, or bones and that your treatment will catch any of those wayward cancer cells and destroy them.

Remember, they gave the cyclist Lance Armstrong less than a 50 percent chance of survival when he was first diagnosed with cancer. We all need to think positively about this. Well, that is all for now. I'll talk with you later.

Love you,
John

Acceptance Is Acceptable

My brother John was instrumental in showing me how acceptance of a life-threatening illness was not only acceptable, but also necessary. Years ago, researcher Dr. Elisabeth Kübler-Ross developed stages for a limited life-expectancy patient. These stages are: (1) denial, (2) anger, (3) bargaining, (4) depression, and (5) acceptance. Kübler-Ross defined acceptance as being "void" of feelings. It is not that the patients give up; it is just a "rest" before the end. Their interests have diminished, and their desires are left in silence. During this time, the family members may need more help than the patient.

Since the time Kübler-Ross first released these benchmark findings, the "acceptance" stage has become more comprehensive and includes acceptance of both the disease and the treatment plan. Today, more and more patients diagnosed with a life-threatening disease are researching the illness through medical journals, books, the Internet, and pharmaceutical companies to learn all they can about the illness and the possible treatment options. They want to have a "scouting report" on the disease so they can beat it.

John recalls that when he played basketball at Ohio University, his coach would come to practice with a carefully prepared scouting report. If a team was good, they had to "overcome" their opponent's strengths. If a team was not so good, they had to "exploit" that team's weaknesses. John's team practiced to exploit and overcome, because on game day they fully accepted the other team as their enemy. They were to be defeated. Accepting the fact that they were the enemy was the beginning of their victory. As John notes:

> The same is true with any life-threatening illness. There can be paralyzing thoughts and emotions when the disease is first discovered, but an individual needs to work at removing everything that hinders a rational and reasonable approach to understanding and treating the disease. The person should bring in a treatment team that not only includes the doctors and nurses, but also family members who can gather information to educate everyone on the disease, suggest treatment options, and offer spiritual and emotional support. Other members of the team may include ministers, church members, counselors, extended family members, close friends, and a support group who will focus on the disease.

John says the goal of the treatment team is to exploit and overcome the enemy. Everyone on the team should be committed to defeating the disease. Everything from pills to prayer should be used, and all members of the team should realize the battle will be ongoing. Accepting the disease as the enemy is the beginning of healing.

January 10, 2007
John,
More updates. We meet with the radiation oncologist today. He is the one I was telling you was recommended by Fox Chase, UPenn, and two other doctors. Both Steve and I liked this oncologist very much. He said that in his thirty years in practice, he can only remember once—a long time ago—when he had a patient with my type of situation. He said that it is not uncommon to have a patient with both breast and endometrial cancer, but not within weeks of each other—it usually takes years.

He said that this is a complicated case, but doable. He will do the pelvic radiation after the three rounds of chemo. He is not sure yet whether he will recommend an implant. He explained the sandwich approach of chemo, radiation, and then chemo again. Like the other doctors, he also was shocked that they had found the endometrial cancer. At one point he commented, "Well, you have obviously had divine guidance in this whole process." Every doctor I have met with so far has been shocked and stunned that there was endometrial cancer, and even more shocked that it was found.

Please don't feel angry over this. That is one emotion I have not struggled with, and I hope it doesn't come later. Feeling overwhelmed, discouraged, confused, saddened, and disappointed are right there in the top five. I usually only break down at home in the privacy of my own bed; however, today I broke down in the doctor's office. The nurse kept trying to get my story straight and write down what I was telling her. The more I tried to explain the situation and answer her questions, the more the emotions built up. I could clearly see that she didn't understand. She kept going back and forth from breast cancer to endometrial cancer and asking for clarification. She almost looked at me as if I were making it up, and the more I listened to myself talk, the more I wished I were making it up. So I proceeded to do what any rational woman would do: I cried. While I wiped the tears, Steve finished explaining the timelines, surgeries, previous recommendations, and the change of plans in regard to chemo.

While I was out walking today, I realized I really have to get a grip on this. There are some givens in life and some things I can do each day. I'm going to figure those out and then return to enjoying life. Of course, this will take time. My life has been totally rearranged. Yet one thing I know I have to do each day is look for God's hand in everything that has happened.

It is interesting that the doctors are all telling me they can see God's hand at work in my life, and yet I'm so distraught I'm not acknowledging it like I should. In fact, since I started this e-mail, I was stopped with a call from my gynecologist. I had called him about a local oncologist recommendation and commented to him that Dr. Coia, the radiation oncologist, had said his catch with this cancer was very good. Without hesitating, my gynecologist said, "I think someone else has been directing this."

Thanks again for being there on the other end. Steve thanks you, too. There is only so much he can hear from me. Today, between all our visits, I saw tears in his eyes. When I asked him about it, he just said he hurts for me. What a guy! I can't imagine going through this without him.

Thanks for your frequent prayers. I definitely know you are praying, because God lifts me up and gives me sanity when I think I am going to lose it. He never lets me get completely down. I know it is the prayers of others that play in that process, because there are times when I am too low to pray.

Love you,
Becky

Get a Grip

For me, part of the fight against cancer and part of accepting my situation was to get a grip on the disease. As children, we had the wonderful privilege of spending time on our grandparents' farm. It was complete with chickens, a garden, and, yes, cows. Now, Grandpa didn't have any of those high-tech milking machines. He was the machine. His large German hands would grip the cow's udder, and in a slow, steady, smooth motion he would draw streams of milk. The best part was the sound of the milk when it first hit the empty pail. You could tell how full the pail was by the sound of the stream as it hit. Every so often, if the barn's cat came around, Grandpa would squirt a stream of the warm milk to the cat to amuse us grandkids.

Of course, as any child would do, after a few minutes watching Grandpa we would beg to milk the cow. Grandpa reluctantly would give up his stool, and we would perch ourselves to deliver the same warm milk. It was harder than it looked. You had to get the right grip, use the right motion, and apply pressure that our smaller, less experienced hands could not do. The cow would stomp, swish his tail, and snort some quick breaths. When this happened, we knew it was time to give the stool back to Grandpa, because he had the right grip.

Cancer forced me to learn the right grip. As part of this process, I not only had to learn to accept the cancer, but also to live each day with the diagnosis and treatments. Bad things happen to people on a daily basis, but nothing could stop my enjoyment of today unless I allowed the fear to loosen my grip on the situation. On most days I could get out of bed, walk, breathe, eat, and talk. I had family and friends to appreciate. I could concentrate on what life could be, not what it should be or what it was before my diagnosis and treatments. Each day, even on the bad days, I had choices on how to invest my time.

Fear weakens our grip, so no matter what situation we may be facing, we must learn to set it aside, strengthen our hands with what can be, and squeeze the udder of life to enjoy the rich warm milk. And don't forget to share some with the cat.

Move on in Life

As I mentioned previously, achievement was part of my family's upbringing. It wasn't that we had to achieve to be accepted, it was just that achieving was a part of life. Maybe it came from the German farm mentality in which we were raised, but work was the main business of life. When we visited Grandma and Grandpa on the farm, we shucked peas, helped wring the laundry through the old Maytag washer, gathered eggs from the chicken coop, split wood, snapped beans, canned tomatoes, and helped bring in the cows.

Now, don't misunderstand: there was time for mischief, or "creativity" as my brother John would have called it. One day, he decided to bring in the cows by firing his BB gun at them. The cows were great targets, but they decided to run away instead of come in. Although John was severely chided for the BB gun incident, he was secretly praised for his initiative. Initiative, ingenuity, and hard work were essentials on the German farm. You were respected for how hard you worked, not how you looked.

To fight the cancer I was facing took initiative, ingenuity, and hard work. Cancer might have robbed my sense of achievement, but it could not keep me from moving on in life.

Thursday, January 11, 2007
Becky,

I am not sure why I am writing to you . . . thoughts of you woke me up at 3:30 A.M. this morning. I prayed for you but could not get back to sleep, so it has been a long day. Maybe you remember how when we were younger you used to keep me from going to sleep for another reason—you stayed too long in that little upstairs bathroom we had in Hazel Park. I think back to those times and realize I had no idea how good I had it—yet I was always trying to move on to something else.

Where do you think we get our proactive attitude from? I think Mother is the travel agent for all my guilt trips . . . any problems I have are rooted in my relationship with her, and any good in me I developed on my own. Of course, I am kidding . . .

Anyway, here are my early morning thoughts. I think the doctors have gotten to all the cancer they know about, and that if there are any cells left, the treatment will destroy them. I also think the cancer should be less energized because you have no female organs and less estrogen to fuel. But the most important thought I had is that God is with you. As I've said before, none of us knows how long we have to live, but I believe you have more days ahead of you. How will you spend them?

As you go through the treatment, I'm sure you are going to feel on some days that death would be a welcome relief. Those are the days to be kind to yourself . . . do not expect too much from yourself when you encounter these times. Continue to read and write. I encourage you to journal all of your experiences. Get your thoughts and feelings (both good and bad) out on paper, list some of the personal goals you have put on hold (e.g., finishing your dissertation), and then look at the calendar and mark the date you will continue pursuing those goals.

During your treatment, set short-term goals for yourself, all the while telling yourself that if you cannot reach a goal, that is OK, and that if you have to modify a goal, that will work as well. The day the treatment is over, or within a couple of days, plan a celebration and possibly even a trip to get away. After each treatment, ask God to keep you cancer free, and then forget about the cancer until your checkups . . . and when the checkup comes back cancer free, praise God and go back to living your life and pursuing your goals.

I have felt from the beginning that God will do something great out of all this, but you have to be the tool that God uses. In his book *Markings*, Dag Hammarskjöld said, "How humble the tool when praised for the work the hand has done."[3] I have faith that God's hand is in all this—your situation is so unusual that God has to be in it in some way, and He has a plan for you in this situation.

Of course, it is much easier for me to say these things than it will be for you to live the experience, but you can do it. OK . . . that is enough for now. I will talk with you later.

Love you,
John

Thursday, January 11, 2007
John,

I needed everything you said. I am coming more to grips with the chemo, although I am scared out of my mind. Both Steve and Joshua think I owe it to myself and to our family to go through the chemo treatments to kill any cancer cells that might be remaining. The doctors have been very honest in saying they are going on the assumption that there might be something there. They don't know. This is the part of the process that doesn't make sense to me. Why would anyone go through something with such serious side effects on the assumption that there might be something there?

Last night when Steve and I prayed together, I asked God to let me live to be an old lady. I hope I don't regret that prayer. I have been journaling, and it helps. I hope someday God will use my thoughts and words to help others. All of your other advice I am holding close to my heart.

Thank you for sharing, praying, and caring. One thing I have learned in this situation is how much I need support. I honestly never thought I would need it this much. Somehow, I naively thought when something like this comes your way, your relationship with God just kind of kicked in and life went on. Boy, was I wrong.

Thanks again for your encouragement.

Love ya,
Becky

I was facing the beginning of my chemo treatments in eleven days. I was scared, but my brother's words had given me the courage to know I could follow our family's tradition: move forward in life and fight the fight.

Keep Pushing the Pedal

Inspired by Lance Armstrong's story, as part my of my recovery I have taken up cycling. Of course, my routine is much less rigorous than Lance's. For my five-mile ride, I leave our house and head east toward Little Egg Harbor Bay, and then turn around and return home. Most days, I face aggressive winds from either the east or the west. I prefer the winds to be from the east, because that way the first part of the trip is difficult, but then the tailwinds push me back home.

Just a few days ago, I decided to make the ride without my husband. I experienced some tough winds on the way to the bay, so I was expecting an easy ride home. But to my surprise, as I turned around the winds coming from the west were even stronger. I had not brought my cell phone, so I knew I had to complete the ride. The wind shook my bicycle, and I debated whether I should stop and wait for my husband to come and find me or face the impossible. However, I was afraid it might get dark before my husband would miss me and start looking for me, so I attempted the ride home.

Each push of the pedal brought almost no forward motion. The two miles home were beyond my capability. Then I noticed that every few feet there were some cracks in the asphalt. So I looked just a few feet ahead and tried to pedal to the crack. When I reached that crack, I set another goal—a puddle, a white spot, a pole—all just a few feet ahead. In between these short-term goals, I thought about the reward of getting home and being out of the wind. It took longer than usual, but within a half hour I was back home, more confident of my abilities than ever before.

When I was confronted with the reality that I would have to undergo chemo, my situation seemed impossible. But short-term goals and modifications equipped me to face the impossible. Whatever you are facing, on the rough days you need to remember to be kind to yourself and let others help you. Make plans for what you will do when it is all over and you can get back to doing the things that you want to do. Enjoy each day, and journal your experiences. Put on your work clothes, don't worry about how you look, and move on in life.

You won't be in the high winds forever, and when you have completed each step along the way, you will be glad to be home and more confident of your abilities. Just take it one step at a time. You can move on in life and fight the fight, even when you are faced with the high winds.

Chapter 5

APPRECIATE THE ENCOURAGEMENT

When I was a child, I could not wait to grow up. However, there are some childhood qualities I cannot give up. Today, I want to be playful, lighthearted, curious, active, and willing to give those I love a big hug.

—John Canine

Psalm of Ascent

A PARANOID MOTHER, an old red station wagon, and a steep road up Lookout Mountain, Tennessee, made for memorable childhood experiences for us kids. Because we had family friends in the area, we made the trip to Lookout Mountain more than once. Climbing the mountain was the climax of the trip. As the car shuddered up the hillside, Mom was never certain it would make it up, and even less certain the brakes would hold on the way down. But survive the mountain we did.

I've often wondered if the writer of Psalm 121 felt this way as he contemplated his journey through the hills to Jerusalem to worship at the temple. The hills looked ominous. Maybe he had a paranoid mother accompanying him, or perhaps the donkey was not sure-footed. Either way, the psalmist concludes that his help does not come from the hills, but the Creator of the hills.

I claimed this psalm shortly before beginning chemo and personalized it to help me trust in God for deliverance. The words of the psalm appear below in italics, and are followed by my personal applications.

I lift up my eyes to the hills . . .

God, this next journey looks impossible. The mountain is steep, lonely, rugged, cold, and dark. There are many pitfalls and places where I can fall and experience harm. I'm scared. I've never faced a mountain like this, and I've always secretly feared this journey. Now I must walk the road up a mountain I have dreaded.

Where does my help come from?

I'm not prepared to walk this mountain. It's too steep, too uncertain. Everyone around me seems to be enjoying life and traveling in the plains. They don't seem frightened of the paths they walk. Even those who support me and stand beside me are incapable of helping me travel this mountain.

My help comes from the Lord, the Maker of heaven and earth.

God, thank You. I was scared I would have to travel this mountain alone, but now I know You will be my help! You are qualified. You made the heavens and the earth. You are almighty. Only You can be my companion as I journey up this mountain. Humanly speaking, it is impossible to climb this hill—but my help will be from You, the God who specializes in the impossible.

He will not let your foot slip . . .

I had expected a slip or two—some scraped knees and injuries as I traveled up this mountain. But You say it is not so. Even when it is rough, You won't let my foot slip.

He who watches over you will not slumber . . .

God, again, thank You. As I look at this journey, I know my human body is going to wear down and tire out. I'm going to be vulnerable. It is at those times I will know You are not slumbering. Thank You, my trusted companion.

Indeed, he who watches over Israel will neither slumber nor sleep.

God, Your promises to Israel are so important. Israel represents Your chosen people. I am grafted in, and I know that You will keep Your promises to me as You have done for Israel.

The Lord watches over you . . .

I was assuming the doctors and nurses would watch over me, but You, God, are much more capable. In fact, if I had to go through this with only doctors and nurses, it would be pathetic, because they are human and have to muddle through information.

The Lord is your shade at your right hand . . .

When it gets hot and unbearable, God, You will give me shade.

The sun will not harm you by day, nor the moon by night.

That takes care of it. I have Your promise You will give me 24/7 protection and keep me from harm. Thank You, God, for mentioning the night, because it is the worst.

The Lord will keep you from all harm.

OK, just in case I didn't get it or it seems too good to be true, You repeat the promise for emphasis. You will keep me from all harm.

Notes, Cards, Phone Calls, and Prayers

Growing up in a religious family, I always had assumed that all you needed in difficult times was God. I had gone to a Christian college where one of the landmark songs was, "Christ Is All I Need." Now, I don't quibble with the theology of the song, nor do I deny that my ultimate satisfaction in life comes from God. But independence is not a good bedfellow for tragedy or hard times. We are not designed to be self-sufficient.

Unfortunately, it often takes a tragedy before we realize how much people love us. When I first learned I had a lump in my breast, two of my friends (Sue, my friend with metastasized breast cancer, and Trish, our school board president who had also had breast cancer) became my "booking" agents. They pretended to be me and scheduled three different appointments for me at three different top hospitals. Later, they called me at school and gave me my choice of appointments. I hadn't even been diagnosed with cancer yet!

When I asked Sue how she was able to give the doctors my personal information, she told me that while she was on the phone with the doctor's office, her daughter was on the cell phone with my husband. When the secretary would ask about the insurance company, she would say out loud, "The insurance company is . . ." Her daughter would take the information from my husband, pass it on to her, and then Sue would give the information to the receptionist. At one point she said, "Her birthday is . . . I mean, my birthday is . . ." at which point the receptionist said, "You are making this appointment for someone else, aren't you?" Sue confessed, and the receptionist commented that people do it all the time. When you are in the midst of problems, you need friends.

Once my cancer diagnosis had been confirmed, the phone calls, letters, and cards began to come. It was like Christmas. Every day I would come home from school and open cards and write notes to people. It was an amazing and humbling experience. I enjoyed the attention and reconnecting with family and friends from the past.

Sue commented to me one day that she never had realized how much people loved her. She told me that she wrote notes back to people and thanked them for their cards. I told Sue I didn't think I had the time to do that. Her comment was, "You have to acknowledge them in some way." I took her advice and began to respond to each communication I received.

The therapy of communication with others was tremendous. During the course of my diagnosis, surgeries, and treatments, I received more than five hundred cards. I responded to almost every one, and each word I wrote brought acceptance and healing. It is the human spirit and support of others that sustains us in desperate times.

Friday, January 12, 2007
Becky,
I enjoy your e-mails. I understand that some days you may not answer, and if I get concerned I will call. Next week, I will be in Memphis, Little Rock, and Miami on business and visiting funeral homes. The funeral home in Little Rock has twenty facilities and receives more than four thousand death calls each year. When I was there in December, I met with the owners and the CEO for their e-team meeting. They started the meeting with a devotional thought and prayer, and the first request to God out of the CEO's mouth was to heal Becky Overholt from cancer! You have people praying for you who do not know you, and you do not know them, but we all know God . . . pretty neat. Sophia is praying for you as well,

although the last two nights she has been too tired to talk to God. I am sure God understands the mind of a six-year-old, and the Spirit makes intercession for her. ☺

Talk to you later. Try to have a good weekend.
Will always love you,
John

One day, I was praying for Sue shortly after she had received her diagnosis. I was feeling overwhelmed with attempting to give her support. I didn't know how or what to pray that evening for Sue, so I prayed God would release His army of encouragers. I did not know where they were or who they were, but I knew God must have soldiers who provided this function. I couldn't get a message to them, but I was sure Sue and her family were going to need them. I knew God could get to these soldiers and give them His command to encourage Sue, so I rested in the fact that He would do just that.

Little did I realize that within just a few months I would need the same army of encouragers. I have since met them, and they have played an important role in my fight against cancer.

Storms and Laughs

As I mentioned, before my chemotherapy treatments could begin, I first had to meet with a surgeon at UPenn about putting in a "port." This port would allow the doctors to administer the chemotherapy drugs to me quickly and relatively painlessly. Steve and I spent four hours driving to and from UPenn and another four hours sitting in a waiting room. Of those eight hours, we only spent about ten minutes with the surgeon.

As I sat there in the waiting room, I told Steve, "This is not how I wanted to spend these years of our lives." Looking around, I was sure no one else wanted to be there as well. I saw sadness, loneliness, and discouragement on people's faces. Few talked, and fewer dared to smile. Many of them were facing their own mortality and their own fears of the ultimate enemy, death. I could understand their blank stares and fearful eyes. I could also see myself in their faces. Where was the joy in life? How could I have joy when my life had been so drastically altered? How could I look forward to the future when I was so genuinely afraid of it?

It was easy to sit in those waiting rooms and let the fear and despair overtake me. I desperately wanted this personal nightmare to end. I longed to get good news and encouraging words from my doctors that the storm was over and they didn't want to see me again until my yearly checkup. Yet, I knew it doesn't always go that way. So I was left to struggle with the joy of the Lord in the midst of the storm.

I don't know about you, but I have never been good at trusting in the storm. I prefer for the storm to end and then praise God because I was spared and unharmed. When our daughter Joanna was young, she frequently came to our bed, especially if there was a storm. One night a terrible Midwestern thunderstorm was raging. Joanna came to our bed, and as she lay there trembling I told her God would protect us. Her faint question back to me was, "Even in the storm?"

"Yes," I told her. "Especially in the storm."

Now my heavenly Father was whispering to me, "I will take care of you, my child, especially in the storm." And I was crying back, "Are you sure, God? Because I'm really scared." This is what I wrote in my journal December 6, 2006, shortly after my second cancer diagnosis:

God, I've been trying so hard to be a good girl—to be strong, read Your Word, write, listen to sermons and Christian music, and practice a "You are my peace, refuge, and fortress" mentality. But I can't do it. I have to stop trying. Tonight I cry out to You and say, "Please hold me. I'm weak. I'm melted. Please hold me, dear Jesus." That is all I can ask. I need You, God. I'm too weak to conjure up faith and belief. I need Your arms of love and strength. I need You to hold me tonight, tomorrow, and all the days of my life. Hold me through healing, through future trials, through peaceful days, and through stormy nights. It's not about what people say. I can't do any more, believe any more, or grab any more knowledge to help me. I just need Your arms of love.

In her book *Hope*, Nancy Guthrie says, "Feeling loved by God is the deep certainty that the God of the universe is not opposed to me, though I deserve it; He is for me. It is an inner confidence in His loving intentions that gives us the security and strength we need for enduring the difficulties of this life."[1]

Yes, God loves us. He created us. Psalm 139:14 says, "I praise you because I am fearfully and wonderfully made; your works are wonderful, I know that full well." We wouldn't even exist if God had not lovingly designed us into being. The simple fact that we are here proves we are worthwhile and He loves us. Even more, Christ's death on the cross to redeem us proves His love. God is not opposed to us, and the difficulties of life need not drive us from Him. This is the time to sing with the children, "The joy of the Lord is my strength . . . He heals the brokenhearted and they cry no more . . . He gives me living water and I thirst no more." And don't forget the, "Ha, ha, ha, ha, ha, ha, ha . . . ha, ha, ha . . . ha, ha" part—even when you are sitting in the waiting room.

Isn't God Like Santa Claus?

John had been out of town on business, so it wasn't until a week later, two days before my chemotherapy would begin, that I again heard from him.

Saturday, January 20, 2007
Becky,
I got home last night. I ended my trip on Friday in Miami . . . I'm tired of planes and airports and people. I got up this morning and had coffee with Nanci, and when we read our devotional and went through the mail, I saw the letter you had sent out to the people on your prayer team. We read the section about "storms and laughs," and that pretty much ended any good feelings we had for the next hour. Nanci and I both cried, and then we talked, cried, talked, and cried some more.

In all the years I have spent in this field of death and dying, I must say I know nothing of what you are going through. Your letter was filled with despair and encouragement, defeat and victory, death and life, body and spirit. I am sure this is what God has for you right now, but as I have said before, I do not like it. You played it by the Book (God's Book) and did all the right things—and you would think people like you who do the right thing should be rewarded and not have to go through a storm like this. After all, isn't God like Santa Claus?

About that "naughty and nice" thing—this brother of yours has not always played it by the Book. There have been times—not many, but a few—when I have left God's road and done my own thing. All those roads were dead ends, and I kept finding myself coming back to God's road. That is where I want to be, and that is the road that keeps me the most content and happy. Certainly, God's road is the road to eternal life.

I have noticed that some people resent the idea of their own death, while others are paralyzed by it. Then

81

there are people like you who have a life-threatening disease and have been given the God-given ability to embrace it and learn from it. Whether you die in three months or thirty years (I vote for the thirty years), this moment for you is significant. The intimacy you feel with God is what each of us wants. We long to have His arms of strength and love to hold us all the days of our lives.

Thank you for your letter, my day is much better because of it. You are truly a remarkable woman. God go with you. I love you and will talk again with you soon.

John

Saturday, January 20, 2007
John,

I know you were joking about God and Santa Claus, but the intimacy with God part is very true. It doesn't matter what our past has been, life is about knowing God's love right now. You may have learned from your roads; I am learning from cancer and the current events of my life. However we get there doesn't matter—what does matter is that we know the love of God that is beyond human comprehension. We have an awesome, almighty, personal God. To know Him is the best.

I am scheduled to start chemo on Monday. Please pray that God will give us wisdom and that He will protect my body. I do not want to have chemo, but for my situation, it is the best medicine available. I feel great and hate the idea of what chemo will do to my body, yet I would have trouble facing my family if I didn't do everything possible to give me an edge on the cancer. It is a vicious cycle. I'm hoping that with good nutrition and exercise, my health will return and God will give me more years. That is clearly His decision.

I love you,
Becky

At my school, there is a student named Howard who has been a challenge since the day he first arrived. As a preschooler, during play time he would often want the toy another boy had, so he would clobber him on the hands, drawing blood and leaving the shocked child with a swollen hand. He has bullied other students, stolen from them, lied, and refused to do his work.

At the beginning of this boy's third-grade year, I asked his teacher, Mrs. Mahr, to schedule a conference with Howard's parents in my office with the hope that we could develop a behavioral plan that would appeal to him. I was sure that if we didn't take action, I would spend most of my days reacting to Howard's antics. This was a last-ditch effort. With the chemo treatments, I knew I wouldn't have the energy to be his disciplinarian. Howard's mother and father took off work and came to the conference. We strategized together, and then called the boy into the office to tell him our ideas. I exchanged cell phone numbers with Howard's parents, and everyone left with a sense that this might be the young man's first good year of elementary school.

Mrs. Mahr carefully implemented every step of the plan and the parents cooperated, and soon other teachers were commenting on Howard's progress. Then one day, the ultimate happened: Howard came to Mrs. Mahr and gave her a dollar he had found. Mrs. Mahr was overwhelmed that he had not spent the money on ice cream or pocketed it. He was practicing good citizenship and returning what he had found. When they got back to the classroom, Mrs. Mahr reached into her drawer, retrieved a good citizen certificate, and asked Howard to come to her desk. She told Howard how proud she was of him and that she was making him a certificate for his good behavior. Howard shuffled his feet and then reached into his pocket. "Well, then, I guess I better give you this one, too," he said as he handed Mrs. Mahr another dollar bill.

We are like Howard. We do a little good and hope it will outweigh the bad we have done. Then tragedy or a traumatic event comes into our lives, and we secretly think our bad deeds must have caused it. We promise to be good and hope the events will change. Yet while God hates sin, He loves us even though we are sinners. His mercies are new every morning, and it is His goodness that leads us to change. Like Mrs. Mahr, He smiles at the dollar we give Him, but He also wants us to give Him the dollar we have stuffed in our pocket.

First Round of Chemo

My first chemo treatment was to begin on Monday. The selected drugs were Cisplatin, Paclitaxel, and Doxorubicin (commonly known as Adriamycin). I was scared beyond description. On Sunday, five deacons from our church came to our house after the evening service and prayed with me. There was no laying on of hands; we simply sat in a circle, and each person prayed. I cried and asked God to protect my body and help me stay strong through the process. When the deacons left, I had a peace that everything was going to be OK.

The next day, Steve and I arrived at the hospital. I was given hydration, a slow-drip chemo, and then the nurse administered the red-colored Adriamycin. The whole process took about four hours. I left feeling perky, went to school, and then came home. At 7:51 that night, I emailed my brother to tell him the good news.

Monday, January 22, 2007
John,
    God literally carried me through my first day of chemo. It was an amazing experience, and I know God

was overseeing the whole ordeal. I was done by one P.M. and went to school and worked for three hours. Then I came home and walked two-and-a-half miles. Last night, the deacons and other two pastors came over and prayed with Steve and me. We asked God for a miracle, and now I feel like the church when Peter was let out of prison. Wow, God, did You really do this? Thank You, God!

I know there will be difficult days ahead, but right now I'm enjoying God's blessing. I just had to let you know. I am feeling a little punk, so I'm going to go lay down a bit.

Love you,
Becky

Sometimes when you are riding the wave, you get slam-dunked by a crashing blow and almost drown in the water. My crash started at two A.M. I began vomiting uncontrollably, and it did not stop. I lay with my head over the side of the bed, losing more than I ever thought I had inside. Every few minutes it just rolled out. The next morning, I was scheduled to go back for the second day of the chemo. I was sick and wasn't sure how they could make me more sick. I grabbed my bedroom wastebasket, which had been my companion throughout the night, and rode back to the hospital infusion center. As I walked in, I asked the nurse when it would get better. Without emotion, she replied, "About the time you're ready for the next round." I began to think, *So much for the success of Sunday night's prayer meeting.*

The nurses let me lay in a bed to receive the Cisplatin. None of the anti-nausea medicines they gave me worked, and I went home feeling sicker than when I had arrived. I don't remember much of the next couple of days. By Friday morning I was back in the hospital, and they gave me hydration and sent me home. On Saturday evening, I was admitted back into emergency. They gave fluids through an IV, and all night long a nurse had to help me in and out of the bathroom. By Monday, I was in isolation. Our son-in-law bought us an inflatable mattress, and Steve camped out on the floor in my hospital room. At one point during the ordeal, the oncologist told my husband he didn't know what to do with me. He had tried everything, but I still continued to lose fluids. He wasn't sure if I would be able to tolerate any further rounds of chemo. I began to think this would be OK because I was sure this first round of chemo had killed everything possible, including me. I came home from the hospital on Friday, ten days after I had started the chemo. Nothing had turned out like I had planned. Why hadn't God answered our prayers?

> *Friday, January 26, 2007*
> Becky,
> Thank you for the update. I pray your faith will bring you through this. I have been traveling a lot lately—five thousand miles just this past week. Just when I think I am living by faith, the airplane will hit some turbulent air, and I realize I am not quite there yet. Faith in God is a total experience, and very hard to do 24/7.
> I heard on the radio a few days ago that one of the area hospitals is establishing a daily exercise routine for their chemo patients. They said it helps to raise the patients' energy level. I do not know what type of chemo they were on, but it sounds like a good idea. Everyone I know who has been on chemo has not had the energy they need. I hope you can keep up your exercise and your journaling. Now is the time to fight with God's strength and power and defeat the cancer with your mind, body, and spirit. What you need is a project.
> Love you,
> John

You Need a Project

Sometimes God answers prayers in ways we do not expect. During one of my worst nights in the hospital, I could not stop wondering if there might be some way that those whom I knew were suffering could share their experiences of hope and encouragement with others. I thought about my friends. Sue had metastasized breast cancer. Another friend had lost her husband to drugs. One was struggling with her teenage daughter, and another had been in an abusive marriage. They each had a story to tell and hope to share.

The next morning, I told my husband I had been up all night thinking about a possible women's conference on God's hope in suffering. He left, and my daughter came to spend the day with me. Sue visited me that morning in the hospital. I told her about my night and the thoughts of having a conference. I asked her if she would be the keynote speaker. She agreed. All we had were two sick people with a dream, but God was ready to intervene.

February 9, 2007
John,

God has answered so many prayers today! I went to the doctor this morning at ten, and I have been out most of the day. This is the first day since Monday, January 22, that I have been able to be out except for my walks around the block, so I wanted to give you an update on where I am right now.

My port is again working for them to draw blood. The whole time I was in the hospital, they had to draw blood from my arm. The doctor who had to work on my port just to get the IV to work didn't know if it would ever work right. He thought I might have to have another one placed.

I gained back five of the ten pounds I had lost while I was in the hospital.

The doctor is recommending that I stay in the hospital for my next treatment, and the insurance company has already approved three days and three nights. They are going to give me a constant anti-nausea IV, hydration, and sedation. I asked them to go easy on the sedation; I don't like to feel out of control.

While I was in the hospital after my first treatment, God put it on my heart that I need to use what I have been through to minister to others in some way. The next day, Sue came to visit me in the hospital. It was the only day I was able to talk even a little. I told Sue my thoughts and asked if she would be interested in being the keynote speaker for a mini-conference for women that we would sponsor. Well, God quickly put things together. Today, we met at Harvey Cedars Bible Conference grounds and set the date—March 25—and planned out the meals, keynote session, and breakaway sessions. Our youth pastor is preparing the brochure.

This is a real step of faith. In December, Sue was only given about eight weeks to live. She was coughing up blood and couldn't even talk. They have since put her on a new treatment. More importantly, God has intervened, and she is up and about almost every day and is feeling well. She can talk and is functioning in pretty much normal ways.

Please pray that God will allow this conference to happen and that He will get much glory from the day. We realize Sue may not have much longer than March 25, but we are still praying for a miracle. He works them all the time.

God is good every day, but this has been an exceptional day of blessings.

I love you,
Becky

P.S. I have a few hairs hanging in there. Not many! The bald part has been fun. Joanna's two boys are quite intrigued. The other day we sat there, and I showed them how Grandma's hair can fall out. They understand and are most supportive. We had to explain that not all medicines make this happen, only chemo. They like the hats, but won't try on the wig. Jessie (he's two) says, "Me no be girl."

Monday, February 12, 2007
Becky,
Your e-mails are truly a blessing. I know I do not have a clue as to what you and Sue are going through and how God is providing His grace for you during this time. The conference is an awesome idea—please keep me posted as to the details and send me a brochure.

Please keep up the exercise. I think I mentioned to you about how Henry Ford Hospital is putting all of their chemo patients on exercise programs because it helps with their strength. Also, I have not talked with Mother in about a week. She was not doing well emotionally—you may want to give her a pep talk.

I have been in and out of town a lot. I leave again on Friday for a week. This one is with the family, so I am really looking forward to it.

I hope you are keeping a journal. Twenty years from now, I want you to sit down with me and go through it page by page—that is, assuming I am still alive. ☺
Love ya,
John

Sacrifice of Praise

The second round of chemotherapy was scheduled for Monday, February 12, 2007. I had been totally unprepared for the devastating effects the first round of chemo would have on my body, so, obviously, before the second round was to begin, Steve and I fervently prayed for a different experience. I prayed God would put His hand of protection on my stomach and work a miracle in my body.

> *Tuesday, February 13, 2007*
> John,
> This is Steve. Becky is in the hospital for the second round. She began yesterday. When I left, and then when I talked with her a while later, she was still doing well. Praise the Lord. No word yet today.
> Steve

> *Tuesday, February 13, 2007*
> Thanks for the update, Steve . . . I am praying.
> John

I was admitted to the hospital and stayed through Thursday so the doctors could administer hydration and IV medicines. God was gracious to me and protected my stomach. I was nauseous at times, but I did not experience the extreme vomiting and dehydration as I had during the first round. What I didn't count on was that "better" would still be bad. Discouragement set in, and I found myself crying out to God. How could I experience such a direct answer to prayer and yet be so discouraged?

For days I lay flat on my back, wishing life would return to normal. Every bone in my body ached. Eating was a chore. Steve had to fix my meals and bring me anything I wanted to eat. I felt like a sick animal, raising my head to get a little nourishment.

Seven days after the second round, I reached a new low. I was reading in the Psalms, looking for verses that confirmed God's love for me. The verses seemed to mock me. I found no comfort, only confusion and disillusionment. There were verses of deliverance—and I certainly had experienced a miraculous deliverance from the first round of chemo—but there was no comfort, no joy of life. I was on my fifth week of extreme nausea, and with the exception of only about three days, I had seen nothing but the inside of a hospital room and my house. Would there ever be any real relief? I wanted to complain to God, but I was afraid that if I complained, my third round of chemo might be like the first. I was stuck. Steve and I prayed, and I cried out something like this: "Please, God, don't be mad at me. I know this time has been better, but I am so low. I can't take this anymore. Please lift me up and encourage me. I need Your help. I'm so sorry. I know I should be praising You and thanking You, but I'm so discouraged. Please help me." The tears flowed.

God then encouraged me with a special verse: "The Lord is close to the brokenhearted and saves those who are crushed in spirit" (Ps. 34:18). There was a promise. I was brokenhearted and crushed in spirit; there was no doubt about that. This verse told me that the Lord was close to me. He had heard my cry.

When I became discouraged and disillusioned, I wanted the ordeal to be over; through, done, finished. I wanted the cancer and the chemotherapy treatments to be behind me, and I longed for the day when things would be like they used to be before the diagnosis. I wanted surface change, but God gave me a deeper truth through Psalms 46–50:

> God is my refuge and strength, an ever-present help in trouble.
> I don't even have to fear if the earth gives way and the mountains fall into the sea.
> The nations are in an uproar, but God lifts His voice and the earth melts.
> The Lord almighty is with me.

I can see the works of the Lord.
God will be exalted among the nations; therefore I can be still and know that He is God.
The God of Jacob is my fortress. God will fulfill His promises to Israel and to me.
He is the great king over all the earth.
He is seated on His holy throne.
The kings of the earth belong to God.
God is my God forever and ever, and He will be my guide even to the end.
The ransom for a life is costly.
God will redeem my life from the grave; He will surely take me to Himself.

Then God told me exactly what to do in my present situation through the words of Psalm 50:14-15:

Sacrifice thank offerings to God,
Fulfill your vows to the Most High,
And call upon me in the day of trouble;
I will deliver you, and you will honor me.

In Psalm 50:23, the Lord went on to say, "He who sacrifices thank offerings honors me, and he prepares the way so that I may show him the salvation of God." I was to sacrifice thank offerings to God in the midst of my disillusionment and discouragement, and God promised that those offerings would prepare the way for me to see my salvation. I am glad that we have a God who understands our weaknesses and that we don't have to be strong for Him. I am grateful that we have a God who understands our discouragement and hears us when we cry. His unfailing love will sustain us in every situation. In every situation, we can offer God sacrifices of praise. Where shall we begin?

Dragging the IV

I don't know if it was John's reminder of what Henry Ford Hospital had recommended for their chemo patients or if was just my personal obsession for walking, but while I was in the hospital I would drag my IV and walk around the nurse's station. The hospital floor was made up of one-foot tiles, and as I walked the floor I counted how many tiles there were from my bed, around the station, and back. There were 165. I went back to my bed and divided 5,280 (the number of feet there are in a mile) by 165, and found that I had to walk around the nurse's station 32 times to walk one mile. That became my project every day. Exercise helped my energy level and gave me something to look forward to. Sometimes I could only go around four times before I would have to lie down, but by the end of the day I always accomplished my 32 rounds.

Thursday, March 1, 2007
John,
Good news! I went to the gym this week on Tuesday and today, Thursday. I did eleven of the machines . . . very slowly and with no weights. It was tough to do, but I felt better afterward. Due to the surgeries, I haven't done any weights since October, so I'm weak. Yesterday, I walked two miles. Praise God for what I can do. I think these things will help.

Don't get too excited about the workouts—one day at the gym, a man stopped me and asked me if he could help me. He said I looked lost. I explained to him that I was on chemo and just had to take time to catch my breath.

My days are filled with the conference and working on my workshop. You were so right. What I needed was a project, and I can truly say that God provided exactly what I needed.
Love ya,
Becky

You just never know from what corner encouragement will appear, but rest assured that if you are looking for it, it will come. God gave me two sympathetic nurses who had experienced chemotherapy, one of whom had just come back to work. Steve and I received notes and phone calls from people to let us know how much they were thinking about us. God's Word was a source of strength, and gospel music ministered to me in the middle of the night. My brother's e-mails continued to uphold me. Exercise gave me a focus other than how bad I felt. As I walked, I was moving forward and making progress. It gave me a sense that I was beating the disease and the medicines' side effects.

Most of the time, my encouragement came from the simple things of life. On some days my encouragement was just the fact that I could still breathe. I also received regular encouragement from my husband. During my weakest days, he waited on me continually. He prayed with me when I reached my lowest points. Early in my diagnosis, I would awake in the middle of the night and find him kneeling beside our bed. I knew he was praying for me.

Look around for your encouragers and enjoy their acts of kindness. When you do, you will begin to realize just how much people love you and the sincere compassion that they desire to share with you.

John, age 5 - Becky, age 1

John, age 9 - Becky, age 5

John and Becky at the after-treatment reunion in Indiana

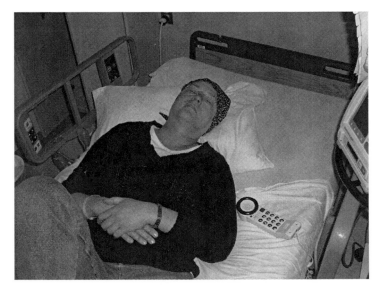

Becky in the hospital during chemo

Becky with grandchildren; Andrew, Allison, Jesse, Matthew

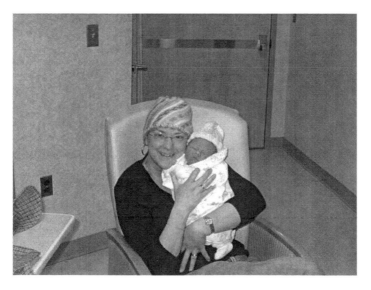

Becky with Jordan, born 10 days after last round of chemo

John and daughter, Sophia

Sue and Becky at the Extreme Makeover Women's Conference
at Harvey Cedars Bible Conference Grounds

Sam, John, Becky, Mom, Pat at the after-treatment family reunion in Indiana

Matthew, Steve, Becky, Allison, Jesse, Mom (Great Grandma),
Jordan (on lap), Andrew at the after-treatment reunion in Indiana

Chapter 6

· ·

LOOK BEYOND THE CIRCUMSTANCES

When we wait in doubt and disappointment for God to do the one thing we demand of Him, we miss seeing everything God is doing and has already done.

—Source Unknown

How Are You Doing?

THE THIRD ROUND of chemo was scheduled to begin on Monday, March 5, 2007. This time, the grandkids joined Steve and me for a little "party." After the first day of infusions, the nurse took me to my hospital room, where I received an IV and sedation. The second day of the infusions, the doctors came and gave me the chemotherapy treatment in my hospital bed. Each round was getting tougher.

Monday, March 12, 2007
Becky,

How are you doing? I know it is a bad question, but I wanted you to know that I am thinking about you and praying for you.

John

Tuesday, March 13, 2007
John,

It's not a bad question. Yesterday was a great day. I worked all day on the conference from my bed. The nausea was bad, but I had lots of energy. It felt as if I were two days ahead of schedule. Then last night my counts dropped, and today it feels like I can hardly wiggle. However, as soon as I am done with this e-mail, I am going to go outside and walk a mile. I just did some exercises on the floor. I just have to push, and sometimes I feel better afterward (if I don't pass out in the process).

This is the first day I have been able to sit at the computer since the third round of chemo began. On the days when I am feeling sick, I just lay in bed—thank God for laptops and paper and pencils. By Saturday, I hope to be able to go back to the gym. Generally, it is amazing how God has protected me during this whole process and how He has allowed me to do so much more than I would have thought possible. I am enjoying basking in His love, which is faithful and true regardless of the circumstances I am facing.

Sue and I have almost two hundred women registered for the conference. I have seventy signed up for my workshop. Sue has her two keynote-session talks ready. When you consider where she was in December, it is a miracle and gift from God that she is doing so well. She is really praising the Lord.

LOOK BEYOND THE CIRCUMSTANCES

Please don't quit praying. I need it, and God is certainly answering many prayers—probably some I don't even know.
Love ya,
Becky

Tuesday, March 13, 2007
Becky,
Your e-mail, as always, was a great encouragement to me. I think it is good that you are pushing yourself with the exercise—keep it up! The conference sounds great. Keep me posted with the information about registration and, of course, the results. Nanci and I will continue to pray for you . . . we care about you and love you.
John

Eternal Glory

Sue and I shared many phone conversations as we prepared for the conference. She knew she was dying. Her cancer was very aggressive, yet God was keeping her alive. As is typical of schoolteachers, we fretted over how the folders were put together and the spelling on the papers in the folders. We hoped there would be enough food for the dinner. I helped Sue finish her PowerPoint presentation for her keynote speech, and she listened to my plans for my workshop.

Mostly, though, we talked about what was happening to us personally. We asked each other why we were working so hard to avoid what we knew would be our greatest blessing: death. Sue was ready to die; it was just that saying goodbye was difficult. She treasured every minute she had with her husband, Howie, her girls, Jen and Noelle, and her grandson, Christian. She longed to live to see the birth of her second grandchild, Elise.

We talked about the thousand-year reign of Christ and wondered where Christ would assign us and what we would be doing during the millennium. I often reminded Sue that even though she might leave this earth, she was coming back with Jesus for the millennium. She reminded me that I must accept what God was doing in my life, because He was in charge of me. She told me I was going to get better, but she would get worse. She planned her memorial service and asked me to speak at it.

Life cannot be enjoyed except through the acceptance of its mortality. Sue knew she was dying, but she fully lived each day. She constantly reached out to others who were sick and met their needs by sending cards, preparing meals, and making phone calls. She wanted God to use her life for His eternal glory.

Thursday, March 15, 2007
Becky,

It never hurts to say, "I feel inadequate." I know it is hard for our family to utter such a statement, but the fact is we all feel inadequate at times. When we admit this, it disarms the people we are speaking with and actually makes them more relaxed.

Remember when we talked about purpose? This ordeal has been so unusual that I feel it has to be of God—He has a purpose that is going to be fulfilled through your illness. I believe a whole lot of people are going to hear about His love through your situation who might not have heard any other way. Of course, there are two ways to look at that. On the one hand, I wish He had chosen someone else; I'm sure you have a lot of other things you would like to be doing besides sharing the love of God through a hairless head and a face swollen from the chemo. But on the other hand, I believe God uses His children to accomplish His work, and their earthly suffering cannot be compared to the eternal glory that will be revealed.

My encouragement to you is to rejoice in the fact that you are a child of God and that He has chosen you to do this work for this moment. His perfect will is being accomplished through you. Not that God asked me this morning, but I believe He has chosen a wonderful woman to accomplish His work, and I pray that this will be the beginning of new challenges for you in ministry—for many years to come.

Having said that, you have given up a lot the last few weeks—and there is more to come—but you are gaining those things that make up the spiritual life, and that gain is for eternity. Perhaps Jim Elliot said it better: "He is no fool who gives what he cannot keep to gain what he cannot lose."[1]

Keep me posted and have a God day.

Love ya,

John

Thursday, March 15, 2007

John,

I'm going for a walk now to ponder some of the things you said in your last e-mail and to pray. I am beginning to understand that God can use this illness for His glory. In fact, it is hard to say, but I'm glad He is using me, even though I have had to endure this cancer. It is all worth it when you sense His presence.

Love ya,

Becky

Broke! Broke!

When our oldest son was beginning to walk, his favorite toy was his popcorn popper. We lived in the parsonage next to the church, and the house had a large kitchen with a white linoleum floor and red curtains. I would wash the dishes, prepare meals, bake, and can vegetables while Joshua played in the cabinet to the right of the sink.

We spent many hours together in the kitchen. The cabinet was filled with Tupperware, which Joshua would pull out, and then he would occupy the empty cabinet as his "cave." When he wasn't playing with the Tupperware or hiding in the cave, he would take his popcorn popper and run it across the linoleum floor. Back and forth, over and over again, he would push the toy to make the little colored balls inside hit against the larger clear plastic ball. All I would hear was *pop, pop, pop* until the sound would stop and Joshua would cry, "Broke! Broke!"

When this happened, I knew the handle had become separated from the popping container. So I would reach down, pick up the two pieces, and then screw the handle back into the popping container. Even then, Joshua would pull it back toward himself and cry, "Broke! Broke!"

How often have we, like Joshua, cried, "Broke! Broke!" and refused to yield our lives to the Lord? Only He can fix what is broken. As Jim Elliot said, wise are those who learn to give up what they cannot keep to gain what they cannot lose.

Time and Space

For centuries, humans have attempted to understand what it would be like to live without the dimensions of time and space. In her book *A Wrinkle in Time*, Madeleine L'Engle tells the story of Meg Murray, Calvin O'Keefe, and Charles Wallace, who are able to transport to another dimension by means of a "tesseract," which L'Engle explains as a phenomenon similar to folding the fabric of space and time. Likewise, in the *Chronicles of Narnia*, C.S. Lewis tells the story of siblings Lucy, Peter, Edmund, and Susan, who are able to travel through a wardrobe to another space and meet all kinds of interesting creatures in a land called Narnia.

Why do our hearts yearn for other-world experiences? Could it be that we are not made for this world because we are eternal beings? Is death simply the doorway to another time and space—something more fulfilling than what we could ever know in this fallen world?

Monday, March 19, 2007
Becky,
I had a few random thoughts I wanted to share with you today. First, cancer is not the death sentence that it used to be. Patients today have many options, and when you combine that with the miracles that God still does . . . well, it gives those who know Him a lot of hope.

We say time is on our side in most situations, but I am unclear on how God sees time—if He sees it at all. God is eternal, and the Bible says God has "set eternity in the hearts of men" (Eccl. 3:11). We know Him in the context of eternity, so we are eternal at all "times"—in space time or out of it. This is why Paul can say in 1 Corinthians 15:55 that death has lost its sting—death only has meaning in the context of space and time.

From God's eternal perspective, death only serves to make us "fully" with Him. Of course, once again it comes back to faith—in believing that everything in eternity with God is better than anything we can find in space and time. This is the core of what Paul says in Philippians 1:20-21: "Now as always Christ will be exalted in my body, whether by life or by death. For to me, to live is Christ and to die is gain."

Talk to you later,
John

Nothing Is as Bad as It Seems

Before I began treatment, John had reminded me "nothing is as good as it sounds or as bad as it seems." I held on tightly to that piece of philosophy during the chemo treatments. There were days when I thought my brother was wrong, but there were blessings every day, whether they came by mail, e-mail, phone calls, visits from friends or family, or God's Word. One of the abundant blessings I received during this time was a good report from Sue's doctors on the state of her health. Life again had possibilities.

Wednesday, March 21, 2007
John,
Sue just called me on her way back from UPenn. They did a lung scan last week, and today they told her that her tumors have significantly shrunk. Praise the Lord. What great news to get right before the conference. I've been crying all afternoon.

Also, I met with the radiation oncologist this morning. He is recommending that I have the fourth round of chemo and the radiation treatment, but not the fifth and sixth rounds of chemo. He said there is no conclusive evidence that anything after the fourth round does much, and he doesn't think I should put my body through it. The radiation treatment is important to fight the endometrial cancer, but it will affect my body's production of bone marrow. To have the chemo after that would risk infection.

The oncologist told me that I am on one of the roughest regimens of chemotherapy. He is really pleased that my body and blood counts have held up like they have. Praise the Lord. I really believe God has protected my body from many things that I probably don't even know. I pray He will protect me during the fourth round.

We now have 339 women registered for the conference, and I have 138 registered for my workshop. The
week has been crazy busy, but I see the hand of God
working in so many ways. Even when I'm tired and can't
do a thing, God intervenes and has someone step up to
the plate to get the job done. It is amazing to watch.
Hope your day is going well.
Becky

On March 25, 2007, Sue and I, with the help of many
people, held the conference we had been planning since just
before I had begun my second round of chemotherapy treatments. John e-mailed the next day to ask how everything
had gone at the event.

Monday, March 26, 2007
Becky,
Well, how did it go? I think your conference was
yesterday. I prayed often for you—I just hope I did not
pray on the wrong day.
John

Monday, March 26, 2007
John,
I've been meaning to e-mail you all morning. I got
up late and just finished reading my Bible. These days I
move a bit slower than before.
God abundantly blessed our conference. Women
came to pray at the end of both sessions. Some were going
through difficult trials. There were many tears and many
happy moments as well. We have already received e-mails
this morning from people whose lives were touched by
the messages. It was truly an amazing day.
Everything worked without a glitch, which, when
I look back at it, is a miracle. It was the Body of Christ
working together in a very special way. You could feel

the Lord's presence as we met and sang and listened to each other. I have never attempted to speak in such a weakened state, but God was faithful and gave me an abundance of energy for my session. It was amazing to see God do that work in my body to allow me to do the workshop. When we were going over to the conference site, I told Laura, Josh's wife, that I didn't think I could stand up and talk the entire time. Sue made it through both of her sessions as well. She was inspiring. I hope to send you some CDs soon.

For me, the most overwhelming aspect of the event was when the women came and talked to me after the sessions. We live in a hurting world. I am weak, and it was hard for me to hear the stories of trials, cancers that have returned, deaths of loved ones, and the intense physical pain that some of these women have endured. They all said they were encouraged by what they heard at the conference, but I felt so inadequate in listening to their stories. It was humbling to have them say God had used us when it seemed that their trials were so much harder. Yet we felt blessed as well, as one of the reasons Sue and I wanted to do the conference was to minister to the many that were hurting.

I start another round of chemo tomorrow. Please pray for me. I'm always a little scared when I do this chemo thing.

Love ya,
Becky

Monday, March 26, 2007
Becky,
Thanks for the update. You have no idea the good you did yesterday. I know that just you and Sue being there gave people hope. Get some rest.

Love ya,
John

110

Tuesday, March 27, 2007
John,
I'm late in leaving for chemo, but I had to tell you three things. First, I was on the phone today with UPenn. The oncologist who I respect very much, Dr. Fox, is on vacation, but he will call me next week about dropping the fifth and sixth rounds of chemo. Please pray that there will be consensus and a peace in our hearts.

Second, I received a wonderful note yesterday from Renata Byler, your business acquaintance. If you see her, please tell her thank you. I won't be able to respond the way I would like for a few days. What an encouragement her note was!

Finally, I am attaching a short piece I wrote for the conference called "The 10 Best Things About Chemo." I used it for the introduction to my workshop. As you will see, not everything is all gloom and doom. I wanted you to have a smile.

Love ya,
Becky

10 Best Things about Chemo

When I was hospitalized after my first round of chemo and sick beyond description, I promised God that if He would help me have my stomach back, I would not complain about going bald. In fact, I told Him I would make it fun. Well, God gave me my stomach back (at least a little), and I began to see that nothing was as bad as it seems—not even chemo.

While I was in isolation—about day seven of the treatments—my hair began to fall out. In a panic, I called my friend Trish and asked her to contact another friend, Carol, who cuts my hair. I asked her to see if Carol would come to the hospital and give me a buzz so I wouldn't drastically notice the loss of hair. I asked my two daughters to be there with me for moral support.

At about eight P.M., Carol showed up and shaved my head. I didn't look in the mirror, but I could see the hair falling to the floor. It was a somber moment. Jodie, my twenty-three-year-old daughter, broke the silence with the biggest grin and said, "Mom, you have a perfect shaped head." Now, if a twenty-three-year-old daughter tells you anything on your body is perfect, it is cause for rejoicing. So I held up the mirror with a smile and decided to celebrate my new look. And as the days went on, I discovered there were many other things to celebrate, which I memorialized in a PowerPoint presentation that I shared with the women at the conference:

> The 10 Best Things About Chemo
> 1. For ten months I didn't have to shave my legs. I could sit and relax in the bubble bath without thinking, *I really need to shave my legs.*
> 2. My daughter thinks I have a perfectly shaped head.
> 3. I got to eat lots of clams. Sometimes you are limited with what you can eat on chemo, and clams tasted good to me. I had more than my fair share of clams—at least three hundred. I've had them for lunch, supper, at my two A.M. feeding and four A.M. feeding . . . anytime I wanted.
> 4. I had time to read cards and appreciate the compassion of those who sent them.
> 5. Things I used to worry about no longer seem important to me—like New Jersey state-required paperwork for schools.
> 6. I know my daughters can take care of me even when I am in isolation.

7. I've connected with my mom, brothers, sister, children, and grandchildren in special ways.
8. Life slowed to a pace I could keep up with.
9. Most days, my companions were Steve and God. I was in good company.
10. I had lots of time to reflect on God's unfailing love.

OK, so I found out there were a few more than just ten "best" things:
11. People noticed my earrings. When you're bald, earrings do a lot for your appearance.
12. Did I mention the cards, e-mails and phone calls?
13. When I showered, the water fell directly over my face, unstopped by soggy hair.
14. I bonded with our custodian at school (he's bald).

There is fun in every situation. Some days, you just have to look beyond the circumstances.

Tuesday, March 27, 2007
Becky,
I enjoyed your humor in "The 10 Best Things About Chemo" that you sent. The real surprise was about Renata's note—I talked to her last week and she did not mention it. She is a wonderful woman. Her family owns twenty-seven funeral homes in Arkansas. They are very active Christians and give a lot to the community. I am praying for this next round of treatment and for the future—which, as you know, is in God's hand. As I've said before, I believe you have a lot more of God's work to do, so rest up for it.
Love you,
John

Friday, April 6, 2007
John,
I'm up early this morning, but exhausted from this last round. Chemo teaches you many things about yourself. I have learned three: (1) I'm a spoiled brat; (2) I don't enjoy suffering and am not very good at it; and (3) I have no desire to learn any more about suffering. All of this is contrary to what God says about the trials of this life.
Have a great Easter with your family. Enjoy the days. Seize the moment.
Love ya,
Becky

Out of the Garbage Pit

One morning when I was undergoing chemo treatments, Steve was getting ready to leave for church. As he was leaving, he told me I would find a card on the couch. I was lying on an air mattress on the floor, angled against our sectional couch. It was my daybed, and from it I had access to what was happening in the house. It also served as a little couch ledge from which to work when I could raise my head for a few minutes.

I was able to find the card around noon (it hadn't been a good morning). On the front of the card in big bold purple script were the words, "You are beautiful," with side comments that read, "regardless of what you do or don't do," "no matter where you go," "even on your not-so-good days," and "just the way you are." (My response to the side lines were, "I am bald," "I don't go much anywhere," "I seldom have a good day," and "I don't do much good for anyone.") Inside the card, not to be overly sentimental, Steve affirmed that humanly I was the most important person in his life and that when he looked at me he was not filled with sympathy, but with love.

Although Steve is human and can fail in his love, what he expressed that day was an example of God's unfailing love. God does not love me because I perform well, deserve His blessings, am good, or have a nice head of hair. In fact, I'm fragile, vulnerable, and, by God's terms, completely useless. I have feet of clay. I don't stand up to God's standards, and I sin frequently. I'm actually good for nothing but the garbage heap. I'm not strong nor self-sufficient, and I do not deserve His favor.

Having cancer and undergoing subsequent treatments has taught me how little I should think of myself. However, it also has miraculously taught me how much God loves me. I am totally unworthy, but God chose to send Jesus to die for my sins so I could be with Him forever. He's brought me out of the garbage pit, redeemed me, and prepared a home for me in heaven. He longs to be with me, to bless me, and to make me happy. He longs to show me His unfailing love. That is amazing love. It is the kind of love I secretly desire, because I just humbly accept it. I do not have to perform or clean up. (In my case that was a good thing, because most days I couldn't perform well and some days it was hard even to take a shower.)

People often ask me how a loving God could condemn people to hell and separate them from Himself for all eternity. I think the more appropriate question to ask is how an almighty God could stoop to love human beings in the garbage pit of life, clean them up, forgive them, and redeem them—all at the expense of His Son's blood, shed on the cross.

We are all condemned. We are hopeless. Look around. It doesn't take a serious medical diagnosis or chemotherapy to reveal that human beings are without hope. But it doesn't end there. For when we are able to see ourselves as garbage, we can begin to know God's love fully. We can bask in His unfailing love that cost Him everything. We can say with the psalmist, "Because your love is better than life, my lips will glorify you. I will praise you as long as I live" (Ps. 63:3-4). We can surrender our lives to God and allow Him to lift us out of the garbage pit. That makes us extremely valuable.

A friend sent me a card with these words from B.J. Hoff, "Lord, help me to stand firm in Your will, knowing I also stand sheltered in your Love, throughout each trial, beyond every struggle, there is Your Mercy, Your Comfort, and Your Goodness."[2] Out of the garbage pit, I am His treasure, even on my low days.

The Spiritual Struggle

One part of being able to look beyond my circumstances was in understanding God's goodness, even when life didn't feel good. One Sunday afternoon when our children were young, Steve and I sat with them and my parents in a Holiday Inn restaurant in Crawfordsville, Indiana. We were home for Christmas. We had been to church with Dad and Mom, and after lunch we were going to visit my dad's sister in the hospital and then head back to Dallas, Texas, where Steve was in seminary.

We shared stories that afternoon, but mostly we soaked up the last few minutes we could be together. Someone mentioned Dad's heart problems, and Mom, being the optimist and encourager, said, "David, I think you are going to live several more years. You are such a good preacher, and God has more for you to do." Dad didn't usually take our German mom on, but when he did he was decisive. He lowered his head, raised his eyebrows, looked over his glasses, and said, "Now, Margaret, God doesn't owe me another day. The fact that Jesus has given His life for me is more than I deserve. If I never live another day, God has been good to me."

Hmmm, I thought. *I sure wish Dad hadn't said that. I like the thought of him living longer.* Four months later, on May 5, Dad died.

No matter how we worship, view God, or practice our faith, it always looks different when we are suffering than when we are at ease. We may think we have deep intimacy with God during the easier times, but there is always a spiritual struggle when suffering comes.

Wednesday, April 11, 2007
Becky,
I just finished listening to all of your CD. You are a good speaker, and the subject matter is relevant. It reminded me of how Rick Warren talks about joy *in* suffering and not *because* of suffering. I believe there is a difference. Your thoughts about Christ taking our suffering and how God wants you to walk this ugly path are so true, though it is a lesson that is so hard for all of us to grasp. No one can or should take this from you. I do not like even saying that, but I know you must go through this to have the understanding of God's love that you talked about and the understanding He wants you to have of Him.

Of course, I also really appreciated what you said about us being eternal. The thought of death can and should unleash within us all kinds of creative, otherworld thinking. Praying for God to show us His love can be dangerous—dangerous because God may show His love to us through means we may not like, such as chemo . . . and sometimes, God may show us His love through His blessings even after we have sinned. Paul said in Philippians 4:11 that he had learned to be content whatsoever the state he was in. Does that mean you should be content during the chemo treatments?

I would like to talk with you more about how the spiritual struggle is harder than the physical struggle. Dad once said to me, "God owes us nothing," but, like you said, we often believe that when something bad happens in our lives, we have done something wrong and God is punishing us. Of course, this makes God nothing more than Santa Claus—rewarding us when we do good and punishing us when we do bad.

Your situation has taken me a lot of different places. When it has not taken me to discouragement, it has taken me to some new creative thoughts. Lately, it has led me to think about the ability of all of us who claim Christ to live outside of ourselves. I am not exactly sure what that means, except that many times self gets in the way of God. Self is to be crucified. Self is to decrease, and God is to increase. It takes self-"lessness" to truly minister to others.

Maybe this is just a thought for me—I am pretty vain ☺. I am sure you did not know that . . .

Love ya, and talk to you soon,

John

Monday, April 16, 2007

Hi John,

This will be a short reply. (Of course, by the time you get to the end of this message, you will realize that I lied.) I am feeling a little better today and can sit at the computer. Praise God for energy. I am praying for more.

Briefly, the spiritual struggle has been in many areas. It has not been easy to find the joy in suffering, as Rick Warren says. Just to find patience and endurance is a formidable task some days. Last week, I found myself beginning to go through the questioning process all over again. You think you have hope and are lifted up, but then the hope is dashed and you are taken down. Even Proverbs 13:12 says hope deferred makes the heart sick. When you feel good, God's promises are not hard to claim. When you feel sick and are just lying there for what seems like an eternity, you get discouraged.

My other spiritual struggle has been in accepting and thanking God for bringing this into my life and not trying to figure out what He is teaching me through it (which I have decided may not always be the primary purpose of our trials). You see, before this happened I was not a perfect Christian, but I thanked God almost every day for what He had given me. I loved my job and prayed frequently about it. If I was in the hallway or a classroom and got called to the office, I would always pray and ask God for wisdom and guidance. I knew when I got to the office I would have to make a decision, and I wanted God's wisdom.

Every Wednesday, I taught our ladies' Bible study. I studied extensively for that and prepared notes and handouts. There were many Wednesday evenings as I drove home that I thanked God for the opportunity to teach the Bible study. I was also enjoying working on my dissertation. I had decided to give it ten hours each week and figured that at that pace it would eventually get done. I had written things to God in my dissertation notebook, thanking Him for the opportunity and asking Him for guidance and direction. Then, almost every night as I lay next to Steve, I thanked God for the privilege of being his wife.

It seemed like I prayed a good deal, and I thought I was doing exactly what God wanted. And it seemed that God was blessing my life. Don't misunderstand: I had the days of guilt where I thought I should pray more and give God more and do more, but I usually thought that they were just that—misguided emotions of guilt. Then when the cancer came, all of the things I thought God approved of were gone, and I had in a very short time a very different life. I'm sure it is similar to the sudden grief many of your clients face. It took me time to readjust to God's new agenda. That was, and still is, the spiritual struggle, especially when I didn't want the agenda I had been given.

You are right about what Dad said. God owes us nothing. I remember when Dad said that to me once, and it left a profound impression. You are also right about selflessness. It is very difficult to say to God, "OK, whatever, whenever, wherever." (Did you know that is the motto of the Special Forces in the military—"anything, anytime, anywhere"?) This is the area of the struggle in which I have most failed God. I told God in college that I wanted to do whatever He wanted, whenever He wanted it, and wherever He wanted it. I still feel that way when I am not complaining about what has been going on in my life these past eight months.

Almost every day, I get cards and letters from people who have either read the Waiting Room letter I sent them, heard the CD, or attended the conference. Sometimes I hear a comment from a church member, like Sharon, who told me that since my cancer diagnosis, she has re-dedicated her life to God and has committed to attending church every Sunday. She has kept that promise. I cry when I hear people tell me that the things I have written or said have blessed them or given them courage. I cry because sometimes I think I only believe what I say or write about 50 percent of the time. The other 50 percent of the time, I am begging God for different circumstances. That is not selflessness. To really die to self, I have to tell God "anything, anytime, anywhere."

So there is the biggest struggle: submission to God. I guess that should not come as a surprise to either one of us. I love God, and I do want to please Him with my life. I don't know how that will work out in the future, but I know that it is what I want. After what I've gone through these past eight months, I have fear in saying "anything, anywhere, anytime." Yet I know that in the Bible, Christ says His yoke is easy and His burden is light (see Matt. 11:30). So why do I fear? I'm not sure. I hate the human flesh and the human struggle. Well, as I said, so much for being short. I must be feeling better. I hope you have the time to read this. Even if you don't, it has helped me to write it. Thanks again for being on the other end.

Love you,
Becky

Tuesday, April 17, 2007
Becky,
I read every word of your e-mail. At times, I am curious as to what my sister's "normal" thinking is (the thinking you had every day for the last fifty-plus years) as compared to her "new" thinking (the thinking you've obtained because of the suffering you've been through). You have insight that the rest of us do not have. I do not say that to inflate you, just to maybe bring some light as to the elusive "why."

I hope you find the proper medium to share your insights. For some reason, this issue of sickness, suffering, grief, dying, and death is paramount in our society right now. I think of the thirty-three families and thousands of people who have been affected by the shooting at Virginia Tech yesterday. The world is very different than the world we knew as kids in Blanchester, but there is one thing that does not change: God.

If Jesus were here today, I am sure He would be on the campus at Virginia Tech, and then after He spent a while there He would journey to Africa to hang out with the HIV and AIDS patients—who are the lepers of this day. Interestingly, attending church would probably be low on His list.

I pray for you daily, and we have a God who hears our prayers.

Love,
John

Friends Don't Let Friends Believe Lies

To think beyond the circumstances of life, we must not get caught up in the lies we are tempted to believe. Five weeks out from my last round of chemo, I fully expected to be perky and free from nausea. Well, it did not go that way. Instead, two weeks after my fourth round of chemo, I contracted an infection, had a 102-degree temperature, went on an antibiotic (which made the nausea worse), broke out in hives because of the antibiotic, and then started on radiation to treat both cancers. Well, if one radiation treatment makes you tired, two radiation treatments leaves you exhausted. I went home from the hospital that weekend feeling wasted and discouraged.

To culminate the weekend, my dear friend Sue Madsen called. As I mentioned, Sue had an aggressive form of breast cancer that had metastasized to her lungs. She had also been feeling lousy, so we shared stories, cried, and confessed to each other the lies that we had been entertaining. We talked about how it is difficult to shadowbox with lies unless you reveal them for what they are—LIES!—and how we never can leave the depths of discouragement until we claim and hold fast to the truth.

As I talked with Sue, I realized I was entertaining a number of thoughts in my own life that did not represent the truth of my situation. So I decided make a list of these thoughts and identify them as the falsehoods they truly were.

Lie One: God Has Abandoned Me

Throughout my health crisis, I had been struggling with feelings that God had abandoned me. This was nonsense. God had heard every one of my pleas for help. He had not abandoned me. As His child, I had the Holy Spirit living within me, so I could never be abandoned, even though I might have felt I had been at times.

The problem was I had established a standard that said God had to answer every prayer my way. When I came to this realization, I asked God to forgive me for forgetting that He was the one in charge and that surrender is always the best reaction. I told Him that He was in control of my life and that He had the right to arrange the days of my life exactly as He pleased. Sue reminded me that He was going to do that anyway, but we agreed that it is for our sake that we need to submit to His authority, no matter what.

Each of us has the Holy Spirit living within us, and He will not leave just because we happen to be having a bad day. If we submit to God and open up to the Holy Spirit's work in our lives, He will minister to us with love and compassion like we have never experienced. This is truth. God does hear us, and He has not abandoned us.

LIE TWO: GOD LOVES THOSE WHO AREN'T SUFFERING MORE THAN ME

Now, that lie was a true pity party. I looked around at those who were not struggling and said to myself, *Wow, wouldn't it be nice if God would do that for me?* God, in His wisdom and love, has the infinite ability to react to each of His children with a personal timeline. We do not need to look at others and compare any of our circumstances to theirs. God is uniquely working out the details of our lives. He loves us and will do what is best for us. He is not a one-style-for-all God.

LIE THREE: I AM USELESS AND A HINDRANCE TO MY FAMILY

I remember one particular morning when I struggled to get out of bed and go to church. *Why should I go?* I thought.

I just fill a pew, and I have no ministries to anyone. Poor Steve tried every approach he knew to get me going as he anxiously looked at the clock. He needed to be at church in a few minutes to preach. I just cried and reminded him I was no good to anyone. But, praise God, I got up and went.

As Steve preached, no one knew what he had gone through to get us both there. And I did just fill a pew. Because I was feeling so weak that morning, I didn't stand, sing, or talk to many people. Yet the music and message were a blessing. God's Word always prevails.

The real truth of the matter is that it doesn't matter whether we are useless or not. Our worth doesn't come from productivity or ministering to others. If I understand Scripture correctly, we are not going to be ministering in heaven; we are going to be busy worshiping God. We are going to fall at Jesus' feet and praise Him for all eternity. We can do that on a lousy day or a good day, especially if we box out the lies and relax in the Holy Spirit's presence.

LIE FOUR: GOD IS MAD AT ME

On many days, it seemed as if God were allowing me to suffer because He was mad at me. But the truth is that God is not mad at us when we suffer. He hates death, pain, disease, and suffering—not us—and He will love us through our trials. He longs to show compassion to us, and He has better plans for us that are literally out of this world. Jesus said, "In my Father's house are many rooms. . . . I am going there to prepare a place for you. And if I go and prepare a place for you, I will come back and take you to be with me that you may also be where I am" (John 14:2-3). Wow! What a plan. We will be where Jesus is.

About two years ago, my cousin Oscar died. When the doctors told him he only had a few weeks to live, he commented to my mom, "Margaret, I've lived my whole life to see Jesus. Now I'm going to see Him." God is not mad at us. Jesus has prepared a place for us. He has not abandoned us in suffering, and He hears our pleadings. We are not useless unless we refuse to worship Him.

God loves us uniquely and will work out our lives for our good and His glory. So even if we are feeling discouraged, we need to get up, and if we physically can, go to church and worship God. We need to live each day with eternity in view, regardless of whether it is a lousy day or a feel-good day. When lousy days pile on top of lousy days, we need to bask in the truth of God's Word, not in Satan's lies. Those will only discourage us and give us a really lousy day.

I am so grateful to Sue for being honest with me and letting me be honest with her. True friends don't let friends believe lies.

Tuesday, June 5, 2007
John,

The more I admit that I am not going to live forever, the more I can accept the possibility of getting bad news. On Sunday evening, our youth pastor preached on the millennium. I turned to Steve and said, "And here I am worried about God giving me twenty to thirty more years here. Wow, am I ever shortsighted."

I had a lousy day today. I had to leave school early and come home and go to bed. I'm not complaining, though, because I realize how much God has protected me throughout the awful treatments. I still got six hours of work in, and I'm able to move about. Some people have it much worse. I just so want to have the energy I used to have.

Have a great day!
Love ya,
Becky

125

Wednesday, June 13, 2007
Becky,
How is the energy level today? I hope you are doing better. I have been in a funk the last few days myself—not depressed (I have seen people truly depressed), but I can't seem to find the positive attitude I need. There just seems to be too much going on right now. When I start feeling sorry for myself like this, I try to think of others who have been through much worse—like you or an attorney I have been counseling who was holding his six-year-old son in his arms at the ER of a hospital when he died of a virus to the heart. Sophia is six, and it is hard not to look toward heaven and say with a scream, "WHY?!"

I really need His grace in times like this, and I really need to believe His strength is made perfect in my weakness. But sometimes I want to kick the cat and punch the wall. (By the way, we do not have a cat, and I would have to fix the wall . . .)
Talk to you later.
Love,
John

Wednesday, June 13, 2007
John,
For me, the "WHY?!" is compounded when I see others struggle with difficult things. I know we are to be submissive to God and He will give us the grace to accept things, but that is what I have struggled with. Frankly—and I've only told Steve this—it has been really difficult to read my Bible and pray the past few weeks. I don't even know what to say anymore. I feel like I am crawling away from getting beat up, and I just want to protect myself. I don't know who or what to avoid or how to cover myself so I don't get hurt anymore.

It is not that I blame God, and I know I have so much to be thankful for, but I have lost more than I ever wanted to lose at this point in my life. Dealing with the loss is difficult. It is hard to believe that our strength is made perfect in weakness. As my strength returns, I keep thinking that the weakness thing was not fun. I fear having to walk through those awful days again. I can't even imagine the pain of the lawyer who had the six-year-old son. Life is hard, or, as our Joshua says, "It sucks."

Sue is not good. They think the cancer may have gone to her brain, and they are going to do a scan. She has been feeling dizzy at times and has problems with walking and her vision. She is still very weak from the e-coli she contracted, but none of these symptoms seem to point to the virus as being the source.

My strength is returning a little more each week. I still have the internal radiation to do. It will probably be next week. I gained one pound. I am enjoying working with the trainer at the gym.

Well, as I look over this e-mail, I realize that it is not very uplifting. So let me close with this: I enjoy each day that God gives me, and I'm secretly looking forward to heaven. I told God this morning that I really want to go to heaven, just not necessarily now. Praise God that He has provided so much for us, both now and in the future. Some day our faith will be sight and these days of frustration will be but a smile. We'll wonder why we ever thought such things, let alone wrote them in an e-mail.

Keep the faith.

Love ya,

Becky

Wednesday, June 20, 2007

Becky,

These are some of my favorite Dag Hammar-skjöld quotes . . . I think you said Steve has his book *Markings*:

"We cannot afford to forget any experience, not even the most painful."[3]

"Pray that your loneliness may spur you into finding something to live for, great enough to die for."[4]

"Your life is without a foundation if, in any matter, you choose on your own behalf."[5]

"Before Thee in humility, with Thee in faith, in Thee in peace."[6]

"The only kind of dignity which is genuine is that which is not diminished by the indifference of others."[7]

"God desires our independence—which we attain when, ceasing to strive for it ourselves, we 'fall' back into God."[8]

"Furnishing this house as your second home is like furnishing a grave-chamber: you know that you will never live here—not after what you have learned. In the old days, Death was always one of the party. Now he sits next to me at the dinner table: I have to make friends with him."[9]

We are going to try to go to Indiana.

Love ya,

John

Thursday, June 21, 2007

John,

If you think of it, please pray for me tomorrow. I have the internal radiation with a catheter. They put a plug in the rectum and a rod in the vagina area. Hate to be so descriptive, but it is not sounding like a nice procedure. They said I would have to lie very still. Imagine that. I can't think of anything else I would want to do with all that going on at one time. I still remember what you said at the beginning of the cancer: "Nothing is as good as it sounds or as bad as it seems."

128

I exercised with the trainer for the fourth time today. It was easier than the other three times. I am getting some strength back. Yeah!

Love ya,
Becky

Power, Love, and a Sound Mind

Chemo has a way of dragging you to the depths of despair. The fear overwhelms you, and you feel you cannot go on or pull yourself out of the downward spiral. In that time of despair, I found that I wallowed in my misery with those whose cancers had returned or who were suffering far more than me. Pain and misery seemed to be the norm, and praying for others was a haunting and daunting experience.

God's Word says He has not given us the spirit of fear, but of power, love, and a sound mind (see 2 Tim. 1:7). Yet I did not always find faith or power within me. Love seemed distant, and fear riddled through my mind like shotgun pellets, killing every bit of peace in its path.

God's work through faith goes beyond the fear or despair we may feel when confronted with chemotheraphy or any other condition. As we read and reread God's Word, our faith miraculously increases and our fear dispels. God does in our lives what we cannot do for ourselves.

We all have an uncertain future, and it is this uncertainty that often causes us to fear. But we do know some things. Let's review them:

- We know God is our creator—our God.
- We know we can trust His heart, even in our suffering.
- We know He loves us.

- We know we have this day to love Him and those around us.
- We know we have this day to point others to Jesus.
- We know we are one day closer to experiencing a blessed pain-free and suffering-free eternity.
- We know we are one day closer to our faith being sight (see Heb. 11:1).
- We know His Word will not fail us and all of the exciting and triumphant things of the book of Revelation will come to pass.
- We know we will see loved ones who have gone on before us. For me, that will be my father and the precious saints of the church. What sweet fellowship we will have!
- We know Satan will be bound and rendered ineffective.
- We know we will be with Jesus for all eternity.

So where does the fear come from? It comes from the enemy. Satan makes us think the here-and-now is all there is, life must return to frivolous normality, and earthly pleasures are all that matter. This is not true. God gives us much to enjoy in this life, but the ultimate adventure is to be with Jesus for all eternity. He says, "Behold, I am coming soon! My reward is with me." We are His bride, and together with the Spirit, we say, "Come!" (see Rev. 22:12,17).

In Revelation 21:3-5, John writes, "And I heard a loud voice from the throne saying, 'Now the dwelling of God is with men, and he will live with them. They will be his people, and God himself will be with them and be their God. He will wipe every tear from their eyes. There will be no more death or mourning or crying or pain, for the old order of things has passed away.' He who was seated on the throne said, 'I am making everything new!' Then he said, 'Write this down, for these words are trustworthy and true.'"

God has promised a new order. Yes, the old will pass away! Death is the doorway to that new order—or, better yet, Jesus' return for His children will be the beginning of that new order. Jesus, the Lamb of God, will be the Temple, and there will be no need for the sun or the moon. The gates of His city will never be shut, and there will be no night. Nothing impure will ever enter, and God's servants will serve Him. His name will be on their foreheads. They will reign forever and ever.

Can you visualize those gathered for the party? There will be Moses, Daniel, David, Joseph, Sarah, and Rebekah, but, best of all, there will be Jesus, who has conquered death, mourning, crying, and pain. Can you hear the triumphant cry of the new order, a multitude of people praising God for all eternity? This will be a party like no other. Many are already celebrating.

When I grasp this reality, I am not filled with fear, but with power, love, and a sound mind. So look beyond your circumstances to the party.

Chapter 7

CELEBRATE THE FUTURE

*If I find in myself a desire that nothing in this world
satisfies, the most probable explanation is, I was made
for another world.*[1]

—C.S. Lewis

Sue

WHEN I FIRST met Sue, she was a kindergarten teacher and I taught fifth grade. It was our fall in-service days, and Sue asked me to have lunch with her. We chatted and found we had many things in common. Before Steve and I had come to New Jersey, her family had attended the church where Steve was pastor. Her husband, Howie, was a deacon, and they had been very active in the church. Church trouble had caused them to separate from the congregation, but they were thinking about coming back.

After one lunch with Sue, I knew we would be friends. She was heady in her conversations and perceptive. She was friendly and compassionate, but not needy. She had many friends, and you didn't have to meet her expectations to qualify for friendship. She was a gifted teacher who knew how to plan events from church parties to school celebrations. She offered practical suggestions for problems.

Over the years, I came to rely on her judgment. As a school principal and a pastor's wife, I often turned to her for a listening ear and solid advice. Our daughters were in each other's weddings, and we supported each other for the planning and implementation of the events.

When Sue received her cancer diagnosis, I was devastated. One night, I awoke during the night and left our bed. When Steve asked me where I was going, I told him I was going to Sue's house to pray. I thought she might be up. I later found out she was, but when I arrived at her house I didn't see anyone stirring, so I sat in the car and cried and prayed for her.

When Sue would see me, she would ask if I thought she was going to make it. She always got right to the point.

Sue was there for me during my diagnosis and surgeries. The night the breast surgeon called to tell me they had found a tumor in my nodes, Sue and her daughter Jen brought supper to our family. She came in the front door as I was on the phone with the surgeon. She sat with me and cried and said, "Oh, Becky, I'm so sorry. I don't want this to happen to you." She knew where I was headed.

A Place Prepared

Sue gave me a great deal of support and encouragement through my surgeries and the chemo. When my treatments were coming to an end, her condition worsened. The last good conversation we had was after the women's conference. We chatted about the event, and I expressed to her how much her family needed her to live. She responded, "No, they will be OK."

Saturday, June 23, 2007
John,
I just received an e-mail from my friend Sue, and I wanted to share it with you. Obviously, I'm crying. There is so much I do not understand in all of this. This is really hard, and yet she moves forward with grace. It is amazing to me.
Love ya,
Becky

June 23, 2007
Dear family and friends,
This is the first time I've been on my e-mail since my last "bulk" letter. I've been feeling really dizzy and unable to focus or concentrate. An MRI yesterday confirmed my oncologist's suspicions—the cancer has metastasized to my brain.

Now, that news is not as bad as it seems. In fact, I think it's a blessing in disguise. As I was talking to Dr. Fox about treatment options, I asked him if it were more difficult to die from cancer in the brain or cancer in the lung. He said cancer in the lung is harder, because you are cognizant and gasping for air. If it's in the brain, you become totally dependent on others, but you sleep a lot. (Sounds like another baby in the house! ☺)

With that in mind, and after talking to my family, I've decided not to have the radiation treatments to the brain. I'll begin a steady decline and look forward to being home with the Lord sometime this summer. Noelle and Elise (and maybe even Brent) are flying in this week. I'll be surrounded by family who will love me and take good care of me. By God's grace we'll get through this difficult time. Please keep us in your prayers.

135

As much as I'd love to see each one of you, give you a goodbye hug and tell you individually how much you've meant to me, my weak, tired body isn't up for any visits. My voice isn't even strong enough to talk on the phone. I want you to know how much I've appreciated your friendship, love, and support over the years. Your kindness toward me and my family throughout my illness has been such an encouragement and testimony to God's love and provision. Thank you from the bottom of my heart!

I can say, like Paul (only because of God's grace), that "I have fought the good fight, I have finished the course, I have kept the faith" (2 Tim. 4:7). Blessed be the name of our Lord!

Please remember me full of life, with a smile on my face and a song of praise in my heart. "I will lie down and sleep in peace, for you alone, O Lord, make me dwell in safety" (Ps. 4:8).

Love,
Sue

Monday, June 25, 2007
Becky,

I was taken away for a few minutes with what must truly be spiritual . . . Sue's words are powerful and show her complete intimacy with God. These are words written by someone whose body is on earth, but whose mind is in heaven. She has packed her spiritual bags and is waiting to go to the home she has thought about and prayed to have—a place Christ has prepared for her. I only pray that someday, given the opportunity, I will die with such grace. We cannot fully understand because our time has not yet come, but in faith I believe God does give grace when we are facing death. This should be a great encouragement to all of us who know Him.

In His love,
John

Tuesday, July 10, 2007
John,

Steve and I are home. We flew in Friday evening. We have had three people in the church die in the last week. Steve had a committal service on Saturday and has two funerals Wednesday and Thursday of this week. You are so right that every day is a gift. Being in Indiana and seeing family was very healing.

Sue is not good. The hospice service has started, and they are keeping her relatively comfortable. Her brother from Germany comes in today. My visit with her on Sunday was difficult; I could see the sadness and fear in her eyes. I don't believe it was a fear of death, but a fear of the process. In weakness, it is hard not to be fearful. We talked about trusting God and how He would not leave her or forsake her even in death. I left feeling so inadequate. How big of me to talk about how God would take care of her. I have not been down the road she is traveling.

Her girls and Howie are sad, but I see God lifting them up. Any way you look at it, as you well know, death is ugly and not a part of God's original design. I'm glad that after we die once here on earth it is not a part of God's future plan for us.

I praise God for my returning health. Each day is a little better than the one before. I think He is going to restore me to health, and I am so appreciative. I'm scared to live, but I'm thankful for life. What a senseless dichotomy. Dee La Foe, one of the ladies at the Monday luncheon, sent me this verse: "The Lord will sustain him on his sickbed and restore him from his bed of illness" (Ps. 41:3). The end of the psalm says, "Praise be to the Lord, the God of Israel, from everlasting to everlasting. Amen and Amen" (v. 13).

Love ya,
Becky

The Best Journey

At the end of July, I went to a follow-up visit with my radiation oncologist, and he informed me he didn't want to see me for a year. Of course, I still had multiple other appointments with my local oncologist, gynecologist, and other specialists, but what the doctor told me during that visit was especially encouraging. He looked me straight in the eye and said, "I believe you are healed. I see no further problems."

Early in the chemo treatments, John had advised me to plan a trip or something else to celebrate the end of the chemo. On some of the roughest days, the advice helped me. I would walk down the street, not knowing if I could make it back to the house, and think about what I was going to do when I was stronger. Would I go to Disneyland? Take a cruise? Visit the Poconos?

Nothing sounded fulfilling to me except seeing my family. I wanted to see my sister, two brothers, and others who had been an important part of my childhood. There was also a group of ladies in Crawfordsville, Indiana, who had prayed for me and sent me countless cards and words of encouragement. I wanted to let them know I was OK and I had survived.

My sister planned a family reunion and party over the Fourth of July holiday to celebrate the end of the treatments. Almost the entire family and extended family came—more than seventy strong.

When Steve and I drove to the farm, we had a sense of anticipation. We parked behind the farmhouse, close to the barn. Pat, my sister, had set up tents, and people already had begun gathering. I was only four days out of my treatments. I was weak, couldn't eat much, and was wearing a scarf, but the energy exploded inside me when I saw the familiar faces from my past—my family members and others whom I knew cared about me.

There was strength in that group. I was home with my people—Indiana farm folks—and for a few seconds I thought this must be what the first moment in heaven is like. That day I spent on the farm was better than any trip to Disneyland. It was better than sitting in a pool or looking at a breathtaking ocean view on a cruise. I was gathered to my people. I was home. I was comfortable. I was finally away from hospitals and treatments . . . and I had lots and lots of family around me.

A Peaceful Home-going

I praised God for doctors who instilled hope in their patients. I praised God for what He had done in my life. I was so grateful to God that He had been with me throughout this ordeal and that I was on the road to recovery. Yet I had a heaviness. I knew Sue's condition was rapidly deteriorating. I didn't know how much longer she had to live, but I knew the time was quickly approaching.

> *Wednesday, July 25, 2007*
> John and Nanci,
> I wanted to e-mail you to update you on Sue's condition. The hospice nurses are keeping her comfortable, but it does not appear she will be on this earth much longer. I started to write she is "failing," but then I wondered why we call death "failing." I also started to write she is not "doing well," but then I realized she will soon be doing better than all of us. In any event, when the hospice nurses were in yesterday, Sue asked them how long it would be, and they told her it could be this week or next week. She told them two weeks was too long.

She sleeps a lot, and I have visited with her some. She is at peace, but very weak. As I have watched her these past few weeks, I have come to believe weakness is difficult to handle no matter how it comes. It is when we are weak that we most need to trust in God. I'm not sure I've learned that lesson. Maybe it is because I still am fighting weakness with everything I have. Please pray that Sue's walk to heaven and entrance to eternity will be a smooth transition.

Love ya,
Becky

Thursday, July 26, 2007
Becky,
Your e-mail, as always, was a great encouragement. I have been lying in bed each night wanting to contact you, but I was concerned that anything I said might take you back rather than forward. In my opinion, we call death "failing" because our sight is limited. The cross represents death, but did Jesus fail? No, quite the opposite—His death became the door to success and victory. Try preaching that for a few Sundays and you probably will not be too popular, but it is true: the entire salvation experience is only meaningful in the context of spiritual and physical death. Take care.

Love ya,
John

Saturday, July 28, 2007
John,
Sue died today at 1:30 A.M. It was a very peaceful home-going. Howie and the girls were with her. She did not gasp for air, but died in her sleep. They sat with her for a while and then began to make phone calls. The family is doing amazingly well. We were with them for some time this afternoon. The memorial service will be Thursday at 4:30 P.M.
Becky

There Is Something to Look Forward to

When the doctors told Sue the cancer had spread to her brain, she knew her time would be short, and she asked me to speak at her memorial service. At the time, I didn't know if I would have the emotional or physical strength to speak. Sue told me to talk about 2 Corinthians 4:7-17, a passage she had quoted to me several times over the phone. Since the time of her first diagnosis, and then when I received mine, she had told me it was going to be OK. She looked forward to every day she had here on earth, and ultimately she looked forward to her journey to heaven. That was Sue's thinking, and it was important to me to capture it in what I said. The following are the words I spoke at Sue's memorial service:

> Those of you who knew Sue know that she could be very directive. She directed classrooms of kindergarten children, and everyone was on task and happy. She was a wonderful teacher. The thing that always amazed me about Sue, though, was her ability to do the same thing with adults. If anyone else tried, they would be called "controlling," but not Sue. Somehow, at a little over five feet tall she could tell you how it should be and you felt as if it were your kindergarten teacher giving you direction. You loved her for her honesty and her ability to give guidance.
>
> Most of you who knew Sue well picked out what you wore today based on her opinion. I sat in the pew today before the service started, and Cathy DiCanto, our former board secretary, said to me, "So did Sue tell you how long you could speak today?" I replied, "What do you think?" In her directions, Sue gave me exactly ten minutes to talk about the passage in 2 Corinthians 4:7-17 that her son-in-law, Tim, read, and somehow I think she meant business. Besides, I'm not in any position to argue

with her, so we are going to try and stick to the plan. The ten minutes doesn't start until now, because she wouldn't have approved of anything I just said.

June 2005 found Sue and the Madsen family at Disney World doing what she enjoyed most—spending time with family. It was at a dinner table in Florida during that time that Tim and Jen announced to Howie and Sue that they were expecting their first grandchild. Two weeks later back in New Jersey, Sue was diagnosed with breast cancer—the beginning of a trial she and no one else wanted. But there was something to look forward to, and look forward Sue did. Their first grandchild, Christian Leeds, was born on January 29, 2006, one day before Sue's last round of chemo.

During the summer of 2006, Howie had surgery, and Sue received news that her cancer had metastasized to her lungs. She began a rough regimen of chemo that made it difficult for her to walk. In her journal on September 20, 2006, she wrote that Noelle, her daughter, and Brent had called to tell her that she and Howie were going to have another grandchild. There was something to look forward to. Sue prayed God would allow her to be with Noelle and Brent during the birth of their baby, and on May 12, 2007, Sue was in Illinois and enjoyed the magnificent miracle of birth and the total love, serenity, joy, and exhaustion on her daughter's face. Elise Frazier entered the world. There was something to look forward to.

My favorite memories of Sue are the talks we had. One evening after she knew her cancer had metastasized, we were talking on the phone and opened the Bible to Ecclesiastes 7:1-2 to clarify what God said about death in this passage. This is what we read: "The day of death [is] better than the day of birth. It is better to go to a house of mourning than to go to a house of feasting, for death is the destiny of every man; the living should take this to heart." As we shared together that evening, we asked each other, "Why do we fight so hard what God says is better?"

Against the backdrop of the birth of her grandchildren was the reality of her death—a reality and trial Sue handled by God's grace. During my own struggle for life, I said to Sue on more than one occasion, "How do you face all that is happening to you? You are a better person than me." To which she always replied, "I can't do it either. It is just the gift of God's grace that He gives to us."

Sue was right. God had illuminated her life through the Holy Spirit and the Word of God. In her college days, she had received the gift of God's grace: the forgiveness of her sins through the blood of Jesus Christ. It is a gift anyone can receive by faith.

In 2 Corinthians 4:1, we read that it is because of this gift of grace that we do not lose heart. Someone wisely said we are either in a trial, just came out of a trial, or are headed to one. Not very encouraging, but the Bible says we do not lose heart because we have a light that shines in our hearts that gives us the knowledge of the glory of God in the face of Christ. This is our treasure, the precious gift of grace through Jesus.

But verse 7 says the treasure is in "a jar of clay." Treasure and clay—the two don't go together. If I had a precious jewel, expensive perfume, or costly gold, I would not put it in a jar of clay. A jar of clay is not permanent, nor elegant, and it is easily broken.

Our treasure is the precious message of God that we can be made righteous through the blood of Jesus. We must give up the notion that we can do anything to please God and simply accept the completed work of Jesus. That is the treasure. It is the treasure of the forgiveness of sin, the treasure of the power of the Holy Spirit, and the treasure of peace with God. Yet the irony is that this treasure is in a jar of clay. The treasure of forgiveness is in a physical body that tends to stray from God. The treasure of the power of the

Holy Spirit is in a body that is helpless. The treasure of peace with God is in a body that struggles with fear and disillusionment.

So we have a conflicting concept—the treasure of God's grace in a weak human body. If the message stopped here, we would have to say, "But God, this makes no sense." However, God soon explains. He gives us this treasure in our frail human bodies to show that this all-surpassing power is from Him and not from us.

Verse 8 says we are "hard pressed." In Greek, the original language of the New Testament, "hard pressed" means crowded, troubled, or afflicted. By God's grace, we may be crowded and troubled, but we are not totally narrowed in or distressed. The power is from God. There is something to look forward to.

We are perplexed. We don't see our way out. In our trial, we do not know what the next day holds. We are at a loss and in doubt, but we are not despondent or hopelessly lost. The power is from God. There is something to look forward to.

We are persecuted, given to suffering. To live in this world is to suffer, but we are not abandoned. We are never left behind. The power is from God. There is something to look forward to.

On May 19, 2007, Sue wrote about several intense trials in her journal. Here is what she said: "Last Saturday, the Lord answered the prayer of my heart. I was in the delivery room for the birth of little Elise. What an incredible experience. . . . I think Noelle's labor (any labor) can be compared to the intense trials in our lives. The pain is excruciating, we want to give up, we long for the trial to end, but we push through knowing (because of our faith in Jesus) that the end result will be invaluable." Elise, invaluable; Christian, invaluable. Just as in the pains of birth there is something to look forward to, so in our trials there is something to look forward to.

By God's grace, we are never defeated. We do not lose. We do not perish. We do not experience permanent death. We push through, knowing the end result will be invaluable and we will be raised up in Jesus. Personal affliction and death is of little consequence against the prospect of the resurrection. There is something to look forward to.

In 2 Corinthians 4:16, we read it again: "Therefore we do not lose heart." Whether you are family or a friend of Sue's, today God's Word says, "Don't lose heart." Sue would say, "Don't faint over my death or your own mortality."

Our jar of clay is outwardly wasting away. Inwardly, we are renewed day by day through faith in Christ and the Word of God. Our light and momentary troubles are achieving for us an eternal glory that far outweighs them all. This is the glory that Sue now knows in person. There is something to look forward to.

A couple of weeks ago, Steve and I left the Madsens' house. I turned to Steve and said, "In a few days, Sue's going to be in good shape and the rest of us are going to be left here to trudge on." So what do we who are left here as pilgrims do? We look forward. As verse 18 says, "We fix our eyes not on what is seen, but on what is unseen. For what is seen is temporary [the things we have around us are only for this occasion on earth, like a paper plate on a picnic], but what is unseen [our faith in Jesus] is eternal."

Sue taught me much in this life. We talked about things such as our church, our school, our families, and our personal lives. She gave me great advice in all areas. I always felt more directed and energized after talking with her. She offered me courage through my own battle, but even more important, she reminded me that life is all about Jesus.

There are many conversations I remember with Sue, but one short phrase stands out. No matter what happened, she always said, "It's going to be OK." It is always going to be OK when our eternal destiny is with Jesus Christ. Though we may struggle through life, by God's grace we can say it is OK. There is something to look forward to. We can look forward to each day, and ultimately to eternity.

Yesterday, Howie and the girls allowed me to read through Sue's journal. With their permission, I want to read Sue's last journal entry dated June 19, 2007: "Karen stopped by yesterday and reminded me that we don't truly start living until we get to heaven. I can't wait to live for all eternity in heaven with my family and friends. Once there, I'll probably be so in love with Jesus, so taken back by His presence, so focused on worship that everything and everybody else will be insignificant. I wonder what heaven will be like?"

There her journal ends. Isn't it interesting that the last question Sue wrote here on earth is now answered? She knows firsthand what heaven is like. She is with Jesus today in paradise, worshipping Him, and everything else is insignificant compared to the surpassing wonder of the presence of Jesus. There is something to look forward to.

We will miss Sue—her energy, her enthusiasm, her wisdom, her graciousness, her love. Howie, you will miss her as your wife. Jen and Noelle, I know you will miss your mother greatly. Ray and Mary and the rest of the family, we extend our sympathy. As special as Sue was to all of us, we know she was even more special to you. Your loss is beyond what words can express. You have demonstrated the grace of God that Sue knew so well. She would be proud of you, and we love you. But for Sue, we must say she has taught us well. She has taught us to keep our eyes on Jesus and never lose heart in trials, because there is something to look forward to.

Come Further In

Sue had experienced the ultimate faith experience. Her faith was now sight. A chapter had ended, and she was experiencing the height of all God had intended in creating her. However, my faith was not yet in sight, and I missed her terribly. Hardly a day went by at school, home, or church that I didn't think about her. We had shared the same oncologist, and at one visit I had told him the reality that Sue was dying was worse than any treatment I was going through. He understood.

When Steve was a youth pastor in Indiana, we went whitewater rafting with the high school group in West Virginia. At one point in the trip, the guide stopped the rafts, hiked us up a hill, and demanded we jump into the deep water twenty feet below. The teens raced to the edge and jumped. I stood back, fearful. Then one of the youth sponsors took my hand. She gave me courage, and with some pulling, I took the leap. I felt a thrill as I plunged into the refreshing water below.

In the same way, Sue has taken my hand in death. Although we have not jumped together, Sue has given me the courage to know that death is the doorway to final victory. It is the entrance into the very presence of God. So as I continue in earthly living, I confidently can say that He who has begun a good work in me will complete it until the day of His return. One day, Jesus will return to claim His Bride and unite us with Him for all eternity. When He returns, Sue, Dad, and others I love will be with Him. What a reunion that will be!

In *The Last Battle*, the final book in C. S. Lewis's *The Chronicles of Narnia*, when the unicorn is entering the new Narnia, he says, "I have come home at last! This is my real country! I belong here. This is the land I have been looking for all my life, though I never knew it till now. The reason why we loved the old Narnia is that it sometimes looked a little like this. Bree-he-hee! Come further up, come further in!"[2]

When that day comes and Christ returns, we will be gathered to our people. We will be home. We will be comfortable. We will be away from hospitals and treatments and sickness. We will be with family . . . lots of family.

Thursday, August 2, 2007
John,
Sue's service was beautiful. I hate for it to be over, because now it seems so final. God did give me exactly what to say, and though I could not get through it at home without crying, I did not break down when I spoke.

Death is so real, and it is not an easy process from any perspective. Oh, how I wish we knew what lies beyond. We say that we do, but it is in such a limited fashion. God answered so many prayers for Sue. She went home gently. God was gracious to her.
Love ya,
Becky

Friday, August 3, 2007
Becky,
The words you spoke at Sue's service will be used in ways that are unknown to us. Every time I think about what you said, I realize the purpose of our faith. God asks us to believe that what is to come will be better than anything we have ever known—without the evidence to give us our own selfish validation. With Sue's journey to Narnia (a C.S. Lewis thought), a chapter in your life has truly ended. But the book is still being written—you have a lot left to say.
Love you,
John

Friday, August 3, 2007
John,
Death is the ultimate faith experience.
Love ya,
Becky

Recovery: Coming Back

When you have been away from your normal routine, it is often hard to return. Others have continued on with their lives, and you have been left struggling on the sidelines. You wonder if you can return to the game. Things don't appear the same, and your perspectives have changed. You don't have the same energy, and you've missed several months of contact with normal living. You might even feel shame about what you have experienced.

It was a summer evening. I had just finished treatments, and the kids, grandkids, and Steve and I decided to go the local Italian ice store. We ordered our desserts and sat outside to eat them. As I watched the other families having fun, moving about with ease, I couldn't help feeling a bit jealous. I still moved slowly, ached, had a foggy head, and wore a scarf. I was tired of being bald and exposing my family to the stares when we were out. I began to think about how different I had made life for them during the past year. I felt so ashamed and wished that my circumstances hadn't happened. My family deserved better than what I had given them.

Monday, August 27, 2007
Becky,
Happy birthday to you, happy birthday to you, happy birthday, dear Becky, happy birthday to you . . . I hope today is your birthday . . . I am not real good about

birthdays . . . I would like to forget them . . . however, most days I am glad that I was born.
Love ya,
John

Monday, August 27, 2007
John,
Thanks, and yes, today is my birthday. It has been an emotional day. When I think where I was at this time last year, I have to acknowledge the regrets and admit the losses. However, overall I am glad to be alive and even thankful that this temporary journey here isn't all there is. I'm looking forward to the millennium and heaven and, Lord willing, some more days of pilgrimage here.
Love ya,
Becky

Shame and a sense of loss still occupied my thoughts, but as time went on, I began to plan for things other than doctor's appointments. I wanted to find my dissertation and finish writing. I began to go to professional development meetings for administrators, and I reconnected with my research partner at Rutgers.

Saturday, September 1, 2007
John,
I have to share this. Today I decided to revisit the dissertation I was working on before the diagnosis. In five hours, I was able to reorganize and get my mind back around it. I reworked my data analysis section and revisited the findings section. I hope to email my advisor some things in the next few weeks.

I am amazed that where I stopped was a great place to reenter the journey. Isn't God wise? Of course, there is not room for too much celebration yet. I know I will be editing and revising and rewriting for several more weeks. That is the way it works at Rutgers, but I am excited about the possibility of continuing. I'm not ready to give up on it yet.

Hope you and Nanci are having a great Labor Day weekend. We are going to Josh and Laura's tomorrow after church.

Love ya,
Becky

Tuesday, September 4, 2007
Becky,

I am so glad you are going ahead to finish your doctorate. Now that the disease has been eliminated from your body, you should be getting back to life as usual—only with a bit more perspective, which usually includes being more loving, forgiving, and patient. I do not mean to sound preachy, but the closer I am to God, the more I desire to be like Him—which, as you know, does not always last.

I tried to get mentally away the last few days, and after four days of doing nothing except swimming, boating, and being with family, I finally looked at Nanci and said:

The days are shorter
The nights are long
Thoughts are simple
Passions are gone

OK, I just had to get that out of my system. I feel better and life is usually good. Whether I am living or dying, God gets the glory. Talk to you soon.

Love,
John

Dealing with the Past

Growing up, Grandpa's green John Deere tractor was a great attraction to us kids. Of course, only my brothers got to drive it—I was lucky if Grandpa even let me sit on it. Grandpa stood six feet tall and had solid muscles, but he had a soft smile. He knew the meaning of work. The day began at dawn and concluded at dusk. Breaks consisted of eating and getting a drink from the water pail. He was a man of few words, and he did not appreciate childish nonsense. We learned at an early age to deny ourselves impetuous behaviors and work hard to get his approval.

One day, I asked Grandpa if I could ride to the fields with him on the tractor. In my childish way of thinking, I thought this would be a great way for me to spend time with him and earn his approval. He warned me I would not enjoy it and that once we were in the field, we would not be returning until suppertime. I brushed off his warnings and insisted I would enjoy being with him for the day. Finally, he relented. Grandma packed an extra sandwich for lunch, and off we went.

The tractor ride was better than I could imagine. I sat on Grandpa's lap, feeling important. The morning wind was fresh and light as it blew through my hair. You could smell the wet dirt and the summer morning. It was everything that I had wanted . . . precious time on the tractor and a day with Grandpa.

A few hours later, the sun, now higher in the sky, beat down on us. There was no shade in the field. On and on we drove. The wind was no longer refreshing, and sweat poured from every pore of my body. Horse flies came out and bit us. Gnats swarmed my head and ears. I hoped we could sit under the shade tree at the end of the field for lunch, but I knew by where the sun was in the sky that lunch was at least two hours away. Complaining was not an option, and a request to return home was impossible. I had only one choice: continue to ride on the tractor as I so enthusiastically had begged to do that morning. Coming back from treatments was not a leisurely tractor ride for me. It meant plowing the fields of everyday living and fighting the sun, flies, and gnats. The treatment had altered my life's perspective, and what I once might have considered leisurely and fun was now work. Yet there was a crop to yield, and I could take pride in accomplishments and steadfast labor. There was fun to be had in the tractor ride, and it was much more fulfilling when I realized how tenacity had helped me "come back" from where I had been.

Saturday, October 6, 2007
Becky,
How are you doing? Is your energy level back to where you want to be? Have you experienced any unusual side effects? Are you to where you want to be spiritually and emotionally? Are you tired of these annoying questions? Just wanted to check in on you . . .

I talked with mother a few minutes ago. It was a difficult conversation. I have lost my voice due to all the speaking I have done recently, and she has lost hers because of a cold. There was a lot of, "What did you say?" I finally ended the call because I was worn out.

Remember, we can't do any of this alone, and God uses everything that happens to us for His glory. That is the deal we call salvation, and in the end I believe it is a pretty good deal.

Love you,
John

Sunday, October 7, 2007
John,

I never get tired of the questions. It is nice to know someone understands that I won't get over all of this quickly. The effects do linger and linger, but I have to say overall I'm doing great. I do not have the same energy level I had before, but I do have energy. Work is getting easier, and I am able to pretty consistently work out and go biking and walking. All of that helps.

Almost everyone is amazed that I go like I do. Yet, I still get discouraged when I think about what my life was like before all this began. My biggest complaint, other than the energy level, is my feet. I still don't have much feeling in my toes, which the doctors say is normal—it is often the last thing to return. That is a minor side effect compared to what I could have been dealing with right now.

Last night we went out to eat with Josh and Laura and the kids. On the way home, we passed the hospital where I had spent so many days during chemo. When we got home and I went into the bedroom (I didn't want the kids to see), I had a major meltdown. All the feelings of weakness and helplessness I had experienced during those days came flooding back, and I again felt so overwhelmed that it had happened. I know that must be how many people feel when something traumatic has occurred in their life. Feelings and flashbacks of emotions are hard to ignore. I am grateful that those moments do not come often now. When I was recovering, they came daily.

Spiritually, I know I love God and that I trust Him with my life and the timing of my death. I love Dag Hammarskjöld's quote about death: "In the old days, Death was always one of the party. Now he sits next to me at the dinner table: I have to make friends with him."[3] I don't mean this to be morbid and I know you understand, but if I get too far away from death, I cannot enjoy life. I do believe I am healed, and I am living with that anticipation, but I also know someday death will be a reality and the doorway to something far better. Accepting death has helped me to enjoy life. Does that make sense?

I want God to use me for the days He has given me here on earth. I'm not sure how long that will be, but I think it is good to enjoy the work He has given me to do now and not always look for something else. I long for the King to return. Everything will be all right when He reigns.

Tomorrow, I go to Rutgers to watch my friend Sandy defend her dissertation. Sandy and I began the study together. We went through data collection and conducted a class at the New Jersey Principals and Supervisors Association headquarters. I was studying leadership content knowledge for literacy, and she was studying the leaders' practices. Last year she was worried that I was moving so quickly I would leave her way behind. Now, she is the one defending her dissertation, while I'm standing on the sidelines. I'm going tomorrow to give her moral support and hopefully to collect some encouragement while I am there that will enable me to finish.

So if you thought your questions were annoying, I'm sure my long answers are even more so. Thank you, though. Communicating with you always helps me to clarify my thinking.

Love ya,
Becky

Monday, October 8, 2007
Becky,

The crying you experienced when you saw the hospital is what we refer to as "environmental cues." These are normal and helpful in that when the flashback comes through the cue, you know you have come a long way from where you began.

The days that I do not have a thought about death are not good days for me. It is scary, but I think God can use anything to minister to others through us. As C.S. Lewis says, we all wait for the return of "Aslan" so Narnia will be restored—when Christ returns, He will set everything right. Now, here is some counsel from your big brother: get your dissertation finished. Just don't feel pressured—remember, it is not the end goal, but the journey that counts.

Love,
John

Moving Forward

It had now been four months since the end of my treatments, and I was just beginning to feel that there was life after cancer. In early November, I had gone in for the latest round of CT scans of my lungs and pelvic area, and the preliminary reports indicated that everything was clear. The nodes were normal sized, and the doctors had no suspicion that there was any further cancer. I was so relieved when Steve read the results to me that I cried for several minutes.

Before that, I had received two good reports from my gynecologist and the radiation oncologist. My mammogram was clear, and my local oncologist had called to tell me all of my blood levels were normal. It seemed everything was truly getting back to the way it had been before I had been diagnosed with cancer. I was again looking forward to working on my dissertation and the possibilities it would open up for my life.

Tuesday, November 6, 2007
John,
Yesterday, I picked up the latest CT scans of my lungs and pelvic area. Steve and I have to go back to UPenn on Thursday to meet with the gynecologist, and we will

be taking the reports with us. However, we unofficially read the disk on our computer, and the written part says everything is clear. YEA! Praise God!

Today I met with my advisor. We discussed the last chapter, and I think I'm ready to write. He said I'm all but finished, but with the holidays we probably will not be able to meet with the committee until January or February. He anticipates that I'll be completely finished by March or April. I'm so distracted by the possibility of finishing that I find myself writing e-mails to you instead of working on the fifth chapter. Concentration becomes more difficult as I near the end.

So needless to say, I am very excited. Against the backdrop of a year ago this week, when I had my second surgery, I have had two really positive days. It is so much easier to praise God on the good days—a confession I hate to admit.

I still struggle with how to make sense of suffering. What I went through is nothing compared to what some people face. I thought about it all the way to Rutgers today. I did not turn my back on God during the whole process, but I didn't worship Him the way that I wish I would have. It was a struggle just to keep my spiritual, emotional, and physical being afloat. Nothing was easy, not even praising God. Do you think most people find it that way?

I often ask myself if I really had the joy of the Lord during my time of trial. It's even possible that I was looking for the wrong kind of joy. There are parts of the book of Job that don't reflect joy, but a struggle. I know God was my strength and my anchor and that He took the edge off of the fear I was experiencing.

These are just some meandering thoughts. I'm not sure life will ever make sense, but I'm sure heaven will. Once again, thanks for listening and for caring.

Love ya,
Becky

Thursday, November 9, 2007
Becky,

Don't be so hard on yourself. I believe that God—though I do not necessarily want to speak for Him—is pleased with how you have reacted during this time of crisis. Think about it: If I ask for patience, do you really think God just makes me more patient? I do not believe that. Instead, I believe He gives me opportunities to learn patience—of which I usually fail miserably at the beginning but hopefully get a little better as He presents more opportunities. I see this in your life as you are learning the joy of the Lord in every situation. By the way, we all need to learn to praise God during the difficult times—we just wish your difficult times had not been so difficult.

I am glad the C-scan was clear and clean; I did expect that by faith. The doctorate is hopefully a given (tongue in cheek), so take your time and enjoy writing the last chapter. Tell yourself you are just going to write a paragraph and see what happens.

While you are having these good days—and from an earthly perspective, you deserve them—try asking God to help you now to be able to praise Him during the difficult times. Just a thought . . . and here's another one I had at three A.M. this morning: How come we do not have enough faith to move mountains? I have to believe the faith is there in our hearts and heads, but how do we tap into it?

I think I have said this before, but I believe that just about everything in our spiritual lives comes down to faith or the lack of it . . . fear interferes with faith.

Talk to you later.

Love,
John

Setbacks

That Thursday, Steve and I went to the appointment with the gynecological oncologist at UPenn. As we walked past the surgical admission door, I said to Steve, "I hope I never have to go through that door again. I'm so glad the surgeries are behind me." All of the reports I had recently received from the doctors indicated the cancer was gone. This was going to be our "happy" visit to UPenn. We hadn't had one of those yet.

Steve and I chitchatted in the waiting room about what we were going to do after we left. We thought we might visit a couple of people from church who were in the hospital, take a trip to Whole Foods, and then spend an afternoon and evening at home, where installers had just put in new kitchen cabinets. Then everything changed.

After my gynecological oncologist finished doing the internal exam, she said, "I don't like what I see or feel. You have a new growth, and with your history of cancer, we are going to have to have it surgically removed and have it checked." I literally got up off the table, looked the doctor in the eye, and said, "You were not supposed to say that. You have got to be kidding." She wasn't joking, so once again I found myself going back through the surgical admissions door, registering for my fifth surgery in a year, giving blood, and getting a pre-surgery EKG and lung X-ray. I was in shock. I couldn't cry or talk. I just stared blankly in front of me.

Needless to say, it was a quiet ride on the way back from UPenn. When we arrived home, I read the last lines of John's e-mail: "I believe that just about everything in our spiritual lives comes down to faith or the lack of it . . . fear interferes with faith." I pondered these thoughts. Fear . . . faith . . . where was I in the spectrum? Up to this time, I had been praising God for healing and renewed health. Was I now to keep the faith and believe that this was just another doctor-prescribed detour? Cancer does come back, regardless of a person's faith. That night, I woke up and sensed God giving me a peace that I was going to be OK. I realized cancer is not a threat to God. He has power over it and any other disease. He heals and restores people to good health, and I was going to claim that victory in my life. He is an awesome God, capable of miracles and the miraculous. He goes beyond modern science and medicine. So I prayed in faith, knowing God was able to overcome the cancer and that if He didn't heal me, it wasn't because I lacked the necessary faith. Healing was not about me; it was about God's power.

My mind was drawn to the story of Shadrach, Meshach, and Abednego in Daniel 3. In violation of the king's decrees, the three men had not bowed to the king's image of gold, and now they were faced with the fiery furnace. Their comment to King Nebuchadnezzar was, "We do not need to defend ourselves before you in this matter. If we are thrown into the blazing furnace, the God we serve is able to save us from it, and he will rescue us from your hand, O king. But even if he does not, we want you to know, O king, that we will not serve your gods or worship the image of gold you have set up" (Dan. 3:16-18).

In the same way, I said to the fear that had returned with this possible bad diagnosis, "I do not need to defend my faith. My God is more than able to handle my cancer or any illness that might affect my body. He can stop it from growing, cure it, and totally take it away. He can rescue me from any danger. Even if He doesn't, I will not bow to the god of fear."

With God, all things are possible. We need not be ashamed of our faith, even when setbacks come, because He is always in control. If we don't get the results we humanly desire, God is still all-powerful. Faith must be our stance. We don't always know what God will do, but we can be certain of what He is able to do. We should not be ashamed to pray in faith.

> **Wednesday, November 21, 2007**
> John,
> My reports are still not posted. I asked the nurse if this was an indication of bad news, and she said no, it just means they are busy and backed up with the holidays. It is most annoying to wait—a word that today has a whole new meaning for me. The nurse promised me that if the results were posted by four P.M., she would call me. That's when they go home. I'll let you know when I hear.
> Have a wonderful Thanksgiving. I am going to be thankful no matter what I hear or don't hear.
> Love ya,
> Becky

> **Thursday, November 22, 2007**
> Becky,
> As soon as you know something, let me know.
> John

Surrender

During the summer of 1968, I took my two nieces and nephew in my mom's green Skylark convertible to swim at a friend's house. We traveled on I-75, a freeway outside of Detroit I often had traveled as I went from Royal Oak to Hazel Park. On this particular day, unknown to me, construction crews had installed a new stoplight at one of the intersections along the route. Of course, I did not see the red light. I sailed right into the intersection and into the path of an oncoming car.

As I realized we were going to be hit, I remember thinking, *Well, this may be it. God, I may be coming home. I'm Yours.* There was a sense of surrender in my heart to what the Lord's will would be in the situation. If I had had longer to think about it, I'm sure fear, despair, or anxiety would have challenged that surrender. All I know is in that instant right before the crash, I understood I was God's child and heaven would soon be my home. There was peace.

Monday, November 26, 2007
John,
I left a message on your cell phone. My pathology report was clear. I called the doctor's office this morning and got a recording that the nurse was going to be out until Thursday. This is the nurse you have to get through to get to the doctor. When Steve came home from church, he made a number of other calls to try to get the results, but to no avail. By five P.M. we still hadn't heard anything.

Then Steve did something smart: he called the after-surgery emergency number. When he got the answering service, they asked him if I was in pain or distress. He told them "distress." So Dr. Chu's fellow associate called. Steve told him I was not really in physical distress and explained the situation, and the guy was really nice. He told Steve my report was clear. There was a polyp (or polyps), but there was no sign of cancer.

Thank God for a good report and a smart husband. I did not want to wait another day. I am very thankful and relieved. Thank you for the emotional support and for caring.
Love ya,
Becky

Wednesday, November 28, 2007
Becky,
Great news!
Love,
John

Since my cancer diagnosis, I have been told I have to fight and that those who keep a positive attitude are the ones who make it. Now if that is true, I'm in deep trouble, and so is anyone else who receives a bad medical prognosis. When you receive news of this nature, there is not much peace to be found, and the struggle can be overwhelming. I'm not sure where you would find this positive attitude, and I was often too weak to fight.

Somehow the answer must be in the surrender to God I felt that summer day when I was about to have a car accident. My life is in God's hands, and no amount of positive thinking is going to change the days He has numbered for me. As the psalmist wrote, "Your eyes saw my unformed body. All the days ordained for me were written in your book before one of them came to be" (Ps. 139:16). Right thinking will only make the days He gives me more enjoyable. God is concerned with my surrender to Him.

There have been many times in my life when I have surrendered to God. As a young girl at Camp Patmos, I went forward to confirm I wanted to do God's will. In high school, I told God more than once that I wanted His will for my life. In college, I knelt in the upstairs room of Milner Hall and surrendered my life to whatever God would have for me in marriage. There was surrender in the decision to work with teens in Erie, the move to Indiana, seminary for Steve, and the move back to Indiana and then to New Jersey. There was surrender when we thought we should minister in South Africa.

Now there is this surrender. It is a tougher and harder type of surrender, because it is not what I humanly want. However, I know surrender is necessary, because if I do not, I will never have another day of joy. I will constantly live in fear, dismay, and anxiety. I will always worry about every medical test I am administered and wring my hands until the results come. If the results are positive, I will have a few days of imitation peace and then return to the "what ifs." The only way I know to have victory is to surrender to God's plan and will for my life, whatever that means. I cannot be absorbed with bad news or the possibility I could die from this complication or some other surprise. When I get those thoughts, I must tell myself God is in control and surrender to Him, knowing His way is perfect and good for me (see Ps. 73:25-26).

The truth is that one day, if Jesus does not return, all of us will die. We will leave this life and go to be with God for all eternity. In light of eternity, does it matter if death happens in two months, five years, or thirty years? The Bible says our present suffering is not worthy to be compared with the glory that will be revealed in us (see Rom. 8:18). Maybe that is why Paul said we need to die daily. I think that until I die to Jesus daily, release the reigns of my life daily, and surrender to Him daily, I never will know the joy of living this day.

Morning Will Come

It was now December 18, 2007, more than a year since I had first so reluctantly walked into the Rena Rowan Breast Cancer Center. As I got off the elevator and approached the waiting room, I saw the same anxious patients sitting in their chairs. Few people had smiles on their faces. Yet for me, the waiting room had become a much different place since that day in September 2006 when I had first walked through those doors. The paths I had taken the past year had taught me many things. I was confident my life was in God's hands and there was nothing that could happen to me that would surprise Him. I had hope in this life and a certainty of eternal life when Jesus called me home. My dear friend Sue had sat in this same waiting room many times. As I mentioned, my oncologist had also been her oncologist. Sue had gone home to be with Jesus on July 28, 2007. Her faith was sight, and her hope was completed. Now she would be having her first Christmas in heaven.

After examining me and reviewing my records, the oncologist told me everything looked good. "You have been through more than most," he said, "but you don't look like you have been through anything." He muttered a swear word and then again asked, "How did we catch the second cancer?" I had no answer to give him other than the one my radiation oncologist had given me: "divine intervention." God clearly had caught the endometrial cancer—no doctor has been willing to take credit for that diagnosis. He has richly blessed me and given me healing. He has restored my life. I have witnessed a miracle in His provisions through the diagnosis, surgeries, and treatments I have received.

As we visited, the oncologist talked about Sue. She had been suffering with a very aggressive but treatable cancer; however, it did not respond to treatment. My oncologist said Sue was a rare person in her faith, courage, and perspective. "I don't see many patients like her," he said.

Had God blessed me more than Sue? No! Had He been good to both Sue and me? Yes! All of our days are numbered, and He writes the stories of each of our lives. Sue would be having Christmas in heaven while I would be having it on earth, but both of us would celebrate it in the presence of our Lord.

At the end of the Chronicles of Narnia, Aslan tells Lucy there has been a railway accident and her father, mother, and all of them were, as they would call it in the "Shadowlands," dead. Then Aslan says, "The term is over: the holidays have begun. The dream is ended: this is the morning." The series concludes with, "All their life in this world and all their adventures in Narnia had only been the cover and the title page: now at last they were beginning Chapter One of the Great Story which no one on earth has read: which goes on forever: in which every chapter is better than the one before."[4]

We are alive through our Aslan, Jesus Christ. The death we fear only has meaning in the Shadowlands. When we step into the light, we realize God has created us to live and the morning is yet to come.

Don't Miss the Miracle

Recently, we picked up our two grandkids in Maryland and traveled to Indianapolis to stay with our other three grandkids. On Sunday morning, we were completing the usual rush of getting everyone ready for church when Andrew, our oldest grandson, remembered he had forgotten his Sunday school paper. I retrieved it from his top dresser drawer and noticed there was one question he had not finished, so we sat on the bed and I read him the Bible story that went with the question.

The story was about the paralyzed man Jesus had healed. As I sat there while Andrew wrote the answer, I wanted to say to him, "I have been healed. Jesus healed me." But I didn't. Was it because we were rushed for time, or was I afraid to say I had been healed? It was probably a little of both. How do I tell my grandson I've been healed if in a few months or years I have to tell him I am sick again? Does God still work miracles?

After my second cancer diagnosis, I began to believe God was going to heal me. I knew it was a miracle that they had even found the second cancer. Yet as I came out of the treatments, it was hard for me to say God had worked a miracle. I was tired and felt as if I were crawling away from getting beat up. I was afraid to say God had healed me. I first had to acknowledge that I had witnessed three greater miracles that were deeper and more significant than the miracle of healing in my life: the miracle of God's grace in suffering, the miracle of death, and the miracle of life.

I experienced the miracle of God's grace in suffering when I was undergoing the treatments for cancer. Due to the chemo, I was in the hospital and sick for significant periods of time, yet in the midst of the suffering I witnessed God's sustaining grace. Suffering is not easy, and each of us dreads the prospect. Yet in our darkest days, God's grace lifts us up and encourages us to continue and persevere. This is a miracle beyond human understanding.

My friend Sue experienced the miracle of death. When we witness a newborn baby take his or her first breath in this world, we exclaim, "It is a miracle!" But when we sit at the bedside of a believer as that person takes his or her last breath, we often miss the miracle that has just happened. I don't mean to minimize the sorrow of those grieving as they say goodbye to their loved one, but death is a portal to eternity—a doorway to the presence of our Lord.

The ultimate miracle is life, and when the miracles come full circle, life is what we will have. God breathed the breath of life into Adam, and everyone who has walked on the face of this earth since then has breathed that life. When our last breath on earth comes, that is when our life really begins.

God created us to live, and nothing can stop that. Through Jesus Christ, we have the miracle of life.

Today, I confidently can say to my grandson that God has healed me. Yet I know that while healing is one miracle, the best miracles are yet to come.

ENCOURAGING COMMENTS

"If I find in myself a desire which no experience in this world can satisfy, the most probable explanation is that I was made for another world."[1]

—C.S. Lewis

I AM FAIRLY confident you are not going to die for a long time.

Time is a most interesting concept. None of us knows how much of it we have, and it does not exist in eternity. I guess that leaves us with the issue of quality. The quality of our time is the meaningfulness of life.

In regard to your cancer, you are going to have a lot of time.

[My neighbor] told me some time ago about his aunt who was diagnosed with breast cancer in her fifties. She had two treatments of chemo and then told the doctors she wouldn't have any more. She lived to be seventy-five.

You are going to live a lot longer than you think, and I am not convinced that you will die of cancer.

Your e-mails are showing to me a deep fellowship with a loving God. I could be wrong about this, but I believe this is what God wants from all of us and, respectfully, I say He does not care how He gets it.

"Let your compassion come to me that I may live, for your law is my delight" (Ps. 119:77).

I believe I know what the peace of God is. I do not always have it, but that is probably the reason I know what it is—and the reason that when I get it, it is so good.

If we were able to take a weekend vacation and check in to our heavenly home, I doubt we ever would check out.

It is never as good as it sounds or as bad as it seems.

Time and God are on your side.

I truly believe God has a lot more for you to do, and without question our lives are in His hands.

In this life we are not going to live forever, but we probably are not going to die soon.

You have a lot of purpose left.

"Fight the good fight of the faith" (1 Tim. 6:12).

This is about you and God and faith.

We all want you to fight hard to achieve full health.

If you worry about dying you will be dead, because you are going to miss life and living.

The things you already have learned are God's gifts to you.

Don't look at the junkyard and miss the beauty of the green grass and the blue sky.

Life is the main business.

They gave the cyclist Lance Armstrong less than a 50 percent chance of survival when he was first diagnosed with cancer. We all need to think positively.

You have more days ahead of you. How will you spend them?

As you go through the treatment, I'm sure you are going to feel on some days that death would be a welcome relief. Those are the days to be kind to yourself . . . do not expect too much from yourself when you encounter these times.

Journal all of your experiences. Get your thoughts and feelings (both good and bad) out on paper, list some of the personal goals you have put on hold (e.g., finishing your dissertation), and then look at the calendar and mark the date you will continue pursuing those goals.

During your treatment, set short-term goals for yourself, all the while telling yourself that if you cannot reach a goal, that is OK, and that if you have to modify a goal, that will work as well.

The day the treatment is over, or within a couple of days, plan a celebration and possibly even a trip to get away.

After each treatment, ask God to keep you cancer free, and then forget about the cancer until your checkups—and when the checkup comes back cancer free, praise God and go back to living your life and pursuing your goals.

"How humble the tool when praised for the work the hand has done."[2]

—Dag Hammarskjöld

It is much easier for me to say these things than it will be for you to live the experience, but you can do it.

ENDNOTES

Chapter One

1. Vittorio Alfieri, quoted in *The Challenge of Living*, John Canine (Birmingham, Michigan: Ball Publishers, 1983), p. 17.
2. C.S. Lewis, *Mere Christianity* (New York: Macmillan, 1952), p. 120.

Chapter Two

1. Leo Buscaglia, *Living, Loving, Learning* (New York: Ballantine Books, 1982), p. 32.

Chapter Four

1. Teddy Roosevelt, quoted in *The Military Quotation Book*, James Charlton, ed. (New York: St. Martin's Press, 2002).
2. Charles Spurgeon, *Sermons from Saintly Deathbeds*, No. 783, delivered December 1, 1867, at the Metropolitan Tabernacle, Newington. www.spurgeongems.org/vols13-15/chs783.pdf.
3. Dag Hammarskjöld, *Markings* (New York: Alfred A Knopf, 1981), p. 140.

Chapter Five

1. Nancy Guthrie, *The One Year Book of Hope* (Carol Stream, IL: Tyndale House Publishers, 2005).

Chapter Six

1. Elisabeth Elliot, *Shadow of the Almighty* (Grand Rapids: Zondervan, 1958), p. 15.
2. Source Unknown
3. Dag Hammarskjöld, *Markings* (New York; Alfred A Knopf, 1981), p. 63.
4. Ibid., p. 85.
5. Ibid., p. 93.
6. Ibid., p. 104.
7. Ibid., p. 106.
8. Ibid., p. 117.
9. Ibid., p. 106.

Chapter Seven

1. C.S. Lewis, *Mere Christianity* (New York: Macmillan, 1952), p. 120.
2. C.S. Lewis, *The Last Battle* (New York: Harper Collins, 1994), p. 196.
3. Dag Hammarskjöld, *Markings* (New York: Alfred A Knopf, 1981), p. 106.
4. C.S. Lewis, *The Last Battle* (New York: Harper Collins, 1994), pp. 210-211.

Encouraging Comments

1. C.S. Lewis, *Mere Christianity* (New York: Macmillan, 1952), p. 120.
2. Dag Hammarskjöld, *Markings* (New York: Alfred A Knopf, 1981), p. 140.

ABOUT THE AUTHORS

Becky Overholt is an elementary school principal and minister's wife. She teaches Bible studies and speaks to many women's groups. After she was diagnosed with multiple cancers in 2006, she helped organize a women's conference at Harvey Cedars Bible Conference Center that gave hope and encouragement to more than 350 women. Becky's authenticity and gift for teaching have ministered to people as she has shared her story with many churches and women's groups. She and her husband, Steve, have three married children, Joshua, Joanna and Jodie, and five grandchildren. They reside in New Jersey, where they have recently joined Global Access Partnership Ministries, working with educators in Southeast Asia.

John Canine is a psychotherapist and the founder and president of Maximum Living Consultants. He is a well-known speaker at national conventions and medical facilities throughout the United States. He has authored numerous books, including *The Golden Postscript, The Challenge of Living, The Psychological Aspects of Death and Dying and What Am I Going to Do with Myself When I Die?* John has three grown children: David, Daniel and Derek. John and his wife, Nanci, live on a lake in beautiful Lake Orion, Michigan, with their two daughters, Samantha and Sophia.

Breinigsville, PA USA
10 June 2010
239567BV00001B/1/P

9 781414 114460